Whose Love Knows
No End

Whose Love Knows No End

A Christian's Life with the Psalms

Thomas A. Sweet

Printed in the United States of America

First Edition 2026

Scripture quotations (unless otherwise indicated) are taken from the New Revised Standard Version Updated Edition. Copyright 2021 National Council of Churches in the United States of America. Used by permission.

Interior design and typesetting by Lori Sweet Studios
Cover Design © by Lori Sweet
Cover Photograph by Eduardo Salvatierra, UK via Unsplash

ISBN: 979-8-9948422-0-1 paperback
Library of Congress Control Number: 2026907735

LionScape Publishing

Harrisburg, Pa
United States of America
www.LionScapePublishing.com
LionScape Publishing is an Imprint of Lori Sweet Studios

Dedication

I have been a pastor all of my adult life. So it is to the many beloveds who have comprised the congregations in which I was raised, served, and who have welcomed me in retirement years that I dedicate this book with deep gratitude. For it is among these saints especially that my life with God and the Psalms has been shaped, nurtured, and encouraged.

To novices it is a beginning; to those who are advancing, an increase; to those who are concluding, a confirmation.

~ Basil of Caesarea

Contents

INTRODUCTION   XI

PSALM JOURNALINGS   1

AFTERWORD   179

ABOUT THE AUTHOR   181

INTRODUCTION

When I consider the aggregate of my life, it is clear that the Psalms, those prayer-songs of ancient Israel's worshiping communities preserved for us in the Bible, have been timeless gifts to me as they have been for many people of faith in every age. While the Hebrew prophets enlighten me in matters of justice, the gospels share the new life offered in Jesus Christ, and Paul's letters and epistles exclaim the joy, responsibilities, and blessings of Christian "community," it is the Psalms that encourage me most deeply in my daily quest to live in relationship with God with faithfulness, compassion, generosity, and love.

While on one level the Psalms are informational, they are most deeply formational. Because all prayer is our response to God's prior move toward us, the Psalms shape in all who read, sing, pray, and attend to them the transformed life to which the prophets, gospel writers, and apostles point us and into which Christians are welcomed in our baptisms. Taken collectively, the Psalms sing our love to God even as they echo the eternal and irrevocable love song with which God serenades us all our lives long.

As we enter into the Psalms, we join Jews and Christians and many others over three millennia who have met in them the *God who acts* in the world and in our own lives. We also come to know ourselves more honestly as we read, pray, and sing them. The importance of the Psalms cannot be overstated in helping us to know both God and ourselves.

That is a great gift for we live in a time when the presence and ability of God to act in this world is doubted widely and deeply. There is a great temptation to reduce God to a religious concept, and we are much the poorer for it. Even the church too frequently uses the *idea* of God to undergird and support its institutional and religious life but without offering any actual or intimate *experience* of God. In the Psalms, however, we encounter a God who is real and actively engaged both in the lives of individuals as well as nations. Through the Psalms, we better come to know our true selves and our place in the world God made and loves.

The other great reality of the Psalms is that, though they are foundational for us as individual persons, they speak primarily of, and into, the divine infrastructure of community. It is within communities and, for many of us, communities of faith, that we live our lives. The Psalms are instructive about how we best and most faithfully can live together generously, justly, and joyfully.

Though a goodly number of the Psalms sing of praise, gratitude, and a well-ordered life, many of the Psalms were born in the cauldron of calamity, the grist of grief, and the heaviness of perceived hopelessness. But no matter their genesis, they never tire of showing us God's way to a newness and a peaceableness that permits everyone - communities as well as individuals - to flourish. Thus are the Psalms particularly relevant to us today.

Then also, of course, both our life in community and our individual lives are set within the context of our earth home and the larger web of life, an indescribable gift and one for which the psalmists expressed continual gratitude, wonderment, and concern. The Psalms are without peer in describing the "necessaries" for a world in which all, everyone, and even the earth itself, can thrive.

The Psalms are a huge and integral part of my prayer life. While I greatly enjoy singing these love songs in the worship of the gathered church on Sunday mornings, I regularly embrace my own discipline of reading and praying through the Psalter. I begin with Psalm 1 and continue on through Psalm 150 over a period of time. Then I begin again.

My own practice is to take ample time each day not only to read and pray the words of that day's psalm but to sit with them for a few moments to allow them to speak through the centuries into my own life today. Through the grace of the Holy Spirit, I sometimes "hear" God in these silent times, informing and deepening my own praying and living.

I heartily encourage you to find your own rhythm and pattern of including the Psalms in your life. What I have found is that, though each Psalm offers its own treasure, it is in the whole sweep of the Psalms that life is transformed. It is in reading them all that each individual Psalm shines more brightly.

Though the Psalms originated within the ancient Hebrew/Jewish worshiping community, I write as a Christian. The Psalms were a bedrock of the prayer life of Jesus and, thus, the Psalms also have become a staple of the Christian church's praying. But they are for all God's people, Jewish, Christian, and otherwise.

This book contains some of my "journalings" as I have prayed the Psalms through the years. These journalings are not meant to be scholarly or formal commentaries on the Psalms. There are many of those already written that are profitable for our instruction. What I offer is simply a modest record of what I have been led to "see and hear" in my engagement with each psalm, a practice I plan to continue all of my days.

I hope they may serve to "open a door" into the Psalms, or to re-open one, in a way that allows you to enter and to make a prayer home in them, too. We do not have to go looking for God. God always finds us. Our praying the psalms nurtures our ability to receive and to welcome into our lives the God *whose love for us knows no end.*

There is a great distance between desiring to pray and actually praying. The Psalms help us to narrow that gap as they offer us a way into praying and, consequently, into a deeper relationship with God and a more profound knowledge of ourselves.

While I am accustomed to using the *New Revised Standard Version Updated Edition (NRSVUE)* of the Bible from which almost all of the brief quotations of psalm-verses and scripture in this book come, please feel free to use the version you prefer. The slight adjustments you will have to make in the wording should be no impediment and may, in fact, enhance your experience.

Thomas A. Sweet
Harrisburg, Pennsylvania
Easter 2026

Psalm Journalings

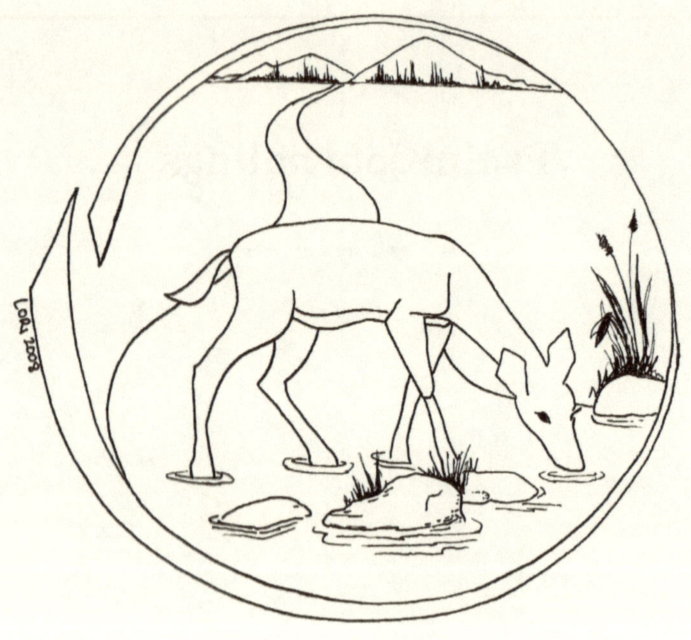

"Psalm 42:1-2"

PSALM JOURNALINGS

In the Psalms, God speaks to us. In the Psalms, we speak to God.

> ~ Thomas A. Sweet

Psalm 1

At the front door of the Psalter, the Book of Psalms, this psalmist introduces us to two ways of living that will be contrasted continuously throughout all of the remaining psalms. One way is to try to live by our own power and wisdom, to make ourselves the captains and arbiters of our lives, and to live with God on the periphery of our consciousness and influence, if at all. It is the way of hubris, arrogance, and, to be frank, functional atheism.

For those who are privileged and advantaged, who are reasonably intelligent, persistent, and clever, this first way can seem to work fabulously, at least for a while. Ultimately, though, it shows itself to be a hollow way, a lonely way, a deceptive way. Even if it produces wealth, status, and comfort, our soul goes largely unnourished as we move along in life, our moral and spiritual growth is stunted, and increasingly we feel far away both from God and a purposeful life. We grow discontented and wither slowly from the inside out as life progresses. True joy eludes us.

The other way to live is to affirm that, first and last, we have to do with God. Being awake and alive to God is in some ways the more difficult of the two paths, even if finally more life-giving, because it requires us to cede ultimate sovereignty of our lives. It requires us to love others, *all* others. Early on, we discern that God's ways and God's thoughts differ from ours in significant respects. Thus, both our perspectives and actions are challenged and we are invited to change. Setting out on the route that affirms God as the center of our lives is the way of humility and hope.

While God's law sometimes is caricatured as being heavy-handed or confining, in reality, it opens us into a lively spaciousness in which we commune with all that is good, just, and noble in life. God does not offer us an easy way but a deeply fulfilling one. The psalmist promises that those who attend deeply to God's law and dare to venture forth in its light will be like *trees planted by streams of water* that thrive and flourish. Though we are not guaranteed luxury by the world's measures, we shall grow rich in the things of God, and that will make all the difference in how we experience life and how we live in the world. Like trees planted beside water, our rootedness in God will enable us to *"yield our fruit in its season"* and to live toward and into our true and full humanity.

Psalm 2

The psalms offer us a prayerful and poetic lens through which we can see life in a way that is near to the heart of God and to the way God intends for us to live and experience it. That way often is called "the kingdom (or kin-dom) of God" or "the kingdom of heaven." Sometimes we call it the "Beloved Community" after the image popularized by the Reverend Dr. Martin Luther King, Jr.

If Psalm 1 shows us that God is the God of individuals, Psalm 2 makes clear that God is also the God of the nations. Even so, the political discourse in our time is replete with conspiracy theories, accusations, lies, and machinations of all kinds as political parties and politicians say and do almost anything to acquire and to stay in power. Sadly, it is nothing new. Nearly three millennia ago, the psalmist in Psalm 2 wondered, *"Why do the nations conspire, and the peoples plot in vain? The rulers of the earth set themselves against the Lord..."*

Misguided politicians and their followers act as if "the earth and the fullness thereof" is ours to do with as we please or to use to prop up our own plans and privilege. We think we can disregard with impunity God's insistence that we practice big-hearted hospitality, care for those who are most vulnerable among us, dismantle systemically-biased systems, eradicate poverty, and steward well the earth.

God's response: *"The One who sits in the heavens laughs; the Lord has them in derision."* No matter what form of government a country employs or what political party is in power, when politics runs amok, when nations conspire to institutionalize injustice while calling it justice, and when the meek and humble do not inherit even the most basic of necessities much less the whole earth as Jesus promised in his Sermon on the Mount, Psalm 2 entreats us to engage reality differently.

The psalmist asks us to hear and to trust the divine assurance that God is powerfully at work in the world and that the Beloved Community is on the way to becoming fully manifest. God's laughter aimed at every claim and effort to the contrary is a comfort to those for whom the way of the Lord, the way of righteousness, justice, and neighborliness, is the precious and guiding vision of their lives.

Most importantly, we are invited to join God in that work for, as Psalm 1 begins and Psalm 2 concludes, *"Blessed are those who take refuge in God and live in God's ways."*

Psalm 3

One of the truly helpful gifts bestowed on us by the biblical psalms is that, as sacred poetry running rich and deep, they may be read and prayed in our time in a large array of contexts, layers, and circumstances. In Psalm 3, David, to whom this psalm is attributed, prays for deliverance from enemies including, the superscription to the psalm tells us, a significant menacing from within his own family.

However, even as this psalm seems on the surface mostly to have enfleshed foes in mind, we also experience "inner demons" who are often as powerful in our lives as any external antagonist, especially when they come at us in the night. While our enemies - outer and inner - may not exactly be shouting, *"There is no help for you in God,"* that is their stridently implicit message as they create chaos in our souls and seek to slay our spirits. They wreak havoc in our lives and threaten our well-being and peace, keeping us on edge, stressed, fearful, and "on the run."

But, just then, the psalmist reminds us of the ever-present companionship of God. *"You, O Lord, are a shield around me, my glory, the one who lifts up my head."* Subsequently, the psalmist exclaims, *"I lie down and sleep, for the Lord sustains me. I am not afraid of ten-thousands of people (or ten-thousands of inner demons) who have set themselves against me all around (and within)."*

It does not usually happen all at once, being liberated from one's mortal enemies or inner demons (such as considering overmuch what other people think of us instead of the graciousness and blessedness with which God sees us in Christ). But it happens increasingly as we seek our refuge, our grounding, our firm footing, in God. That is one of the great benefits to us of regularly reading and praying the Psalms and taking them to heart.

We cannot find relief or security by eliminating our enemies, whoever or whatever they may be, because there always will be more of them. We do not, if we are wise, exact revenge or perpetrate violence against our physical enemies and we do not deny or suppress our inner tormenters. Rather, our deliverance, restoration, and strength for the way ahead are revealed and gifted to us again and again as we trust God to meet us in our need!

Psalm 4

This psalmist is more than a little troubled by the treacherous actions of people who seek to justify themselves and their decisions by denigrating him.

Those who gossip about us, wrongly accuse us, or demean or diminish us for their own reputational, financial, or influential gain evoke a visceral response in us. Our default reaction is to get angry with our tormentors and to strike back in some manner, to get even. But the psalmist says, *"When you are disturbed or outraged, do not sin; ponder it on your beds, and be silent. Offer right sacrifices (read: worship, pray, serve) and put your trust in the Lord."* Easier said than done, yes, but it is the far wiser course.

Meeting aggression with aggression of our own almost never works no matter whether it is of the physical or emotional/spiritual/psychological variety. Do not make things worse by ratcheting up tensions or returning evil for evil. Do not allow the actions of others to fill your heart with malice. The psalmist counsels us to remember who we are in the sight of God - we are God's beloved - and to take refuge and solace in God's steadfast love for us.

While our inclination is to get worked up about disrespect hurled our way, the psalmist advises silence. The psalmist knows the Lord is most apt to be heard *"not in earthquake or fire, but in the still, small voice."* Because, as the apostle Paul later explained, *"Christ prays in us and for us,"* we do well to listen in quietude to what God is "saying" in us, to us, and through us in these difficult situations.

While a challenge for us at first, as we handle ourselves as the psalmist suggests - refraining from returning rant and cant at our antagonists either physically or verbally while instead "taking it to the Lord in prayer" - we shall experience God *"putting gladness in our hearts."* Then, at the end of the day, we shall *"lie down and sleep in peace,"* a great gift.

Psalm 5

The psalms seldom traffic in flowery language and polite thoughts. Indeed, like Psalm 5, they can be rough and raw.

In Psalm 5, the psalmist excoriates those whose falsehoods threaten both the common life of the faithful and the personal lives of the righteous. The Psalms remind us that the righteous and faithful are not "perfect people" but those who are oriented toward God and God's ways in the world. They are those who trust, love, hope in, and depend on the grace of God and who are desirous of living in fidelity to God's ways on the earth. The "wicked" are those who do not and are not.

Contemporary life makes this psalm particularly germane in the face of people and politicians whose lies about science, history, election fraud, racism, the gospel of Jesus Christ, and human responsibility for climate change endanger our collective and planetary well-being. We also experience prevarications proffered against us personally that seek to undo and discredit us to the falsifiers' advantage.

The psalmist says of the equivocators: *"There is no truth in their mouths; their hearts are destruction…Make them bear their guilt, O God; let them fall by their own counsels…"*

The psalmist also prays that he and the faithful not respond in kind to those who speak falsely with lies and bad behavior of their own: *"Lead me in your righteousness, O Lord."*

We do not have to sanitize our prayer for God's benefit. Indeed, soft-selling our situations or sentiments isn't satisfactory on any account for it underestimates the power and desire of God to heal and reconcile in even the hardest conditions and harshest circumstances.

"Listen to my words, O Lord," the psalmist pleads in Psalm 5. *"Attend to my sighing."* Those things God certainly will do. But, then, let us also do the same. Let us listen well to the Spirit of God and follow in God's way for that is how the kingdom (kin-dom) of God, the Beloved Community, comes to expression and fruition in our lives and in the world.

Psalm 6

The psalmist knows that God is the greatest reality of his life. He fully believes that whatever happens to him happens within the all-encompassing reality and presence of God even when he doesn't fully understand. (In Paul's "hymn to love" in 1 Corinthians 13, he writes, *"Now we see only a reflection, as in a mirror, dimly, but then we shall see as face to face. Now I know only in part, then I will know fully, even as I have been fully known."*) It doesn't mean the psalmist never questions God. It doesn't mean he never struggles with the hard edges and heartaches of life.

The psalmist cannot always make sense of God's ways but has determined always to be honest with God. *"Don't get angry with me, God. I'm languishing. I'm not well. Every night I cry myself to sleep and fret and worry. Why? How long, O Lord? Are you going to do something?"* We don't know whether the psalmist is suffering from a medical malady, spiritual malaise, malice from enemies, or a crisis of the spirit. No matter the reason, the psalmist is desperate for relief.

We know whereof the psalmist speaks, do we not? We all have experienced our own versions of the psalmist's sobering and disturbing plight. Hasn't each of us endured intense physical suffering, mental anguish, or grief within our soul? Haven't all of us been wracked with worry in the night or encumbered by the enmity of others by day?

As the psalmist's prayer life deepened, and he spent as much or more time listening for God's "voice" speaking to him as he did speaking to God, the psalmist came to accept what theologians call "the providence of God." So can we: nothing occurs outside of the purview of God. That doesn't mean God directly causes everything that happens but it does mean we are never alone, that God will not leave us comfortless, that God is with us always, and that in every situation God is working God's good purposes out.

"The Lord has heard the sound of my weeping and my supplication and accepts my prayer." In the end, the psalmist was reassured that his life is inextricably and eternally wrapped in God. That "in-the-bones" knowledge became more important to him than any particular outcome to his present situation because he knew he can trust God wholly. He can trust God wholly! And that great gift became the gracious answer to the psalmist's prayer.

Psalm 7

Mostly we do not object to being judged or punished for our thoughts and actions when we know we have erred, slipped up, missed the mark, or, in biblical parlance, sinned. We accept that we are not perfect and, like St. Paul in Romans 7:15, we can confess that *"sometimes I do not do what I want, but I do the very thing I hate."* We can take our reproof in stride and determine to learn our lesson and perhaps become a better person for it all.

We do not fear God's judgment, either, because *"God's judgment goes forth as the light"* (Hosea 6:5) and is wrapped in grace. God's judgment is not for the purpose of condemnation, but restoration; not for annihilation, but salvation.

What really chafes this psalmist (David) is when accusations and disparagements are directed at him unfairly or unjustly by others projecting their own "stuff" onto him. (David had defeated Goliath, his victory bringing relief for Israel in its conflict with the Philistines. And David's beautiful music frequently had comforted King Saul's tortured soul. Even so, Saul inexplicably and unjustly "had it in" for David and attempted even to have him killed.) The psalmist objects stridently to being persecuted for *unrighteousness'* sake.

When that happens to us personally, there often is little to be done because our accusers typically are not ready to hear our objections. Usually persons speaking or acting unjustly against others are unhappy with their own lives, or are conflicted internally, or believe the lies they tell themselves. They strike out at those whose lives seem to hold the coherence and calm they jealously desire for themselves. The psalmist says that eventually the antagonists and troublemakers will *"fall into the hole they themselves have dug"* and *"their mischief will return upon their own heads."*

But, because we do not wish ill on others (even though, as the psalmists often did, we may blow off steam by expressing our deep exasperation with our "enemies" and suggesting to God what God might do with them), this is a good place to practice the admonition of St. Paul to *"bless those who persecute you; bless and do not curse them."* If God's judgments are kindly given, perhaps ours can be, too, even while observing appropriate boundaries. (There is no need to facilitate others in using us as doormats, for instance, or perpetuating abuse against us.) Like the psalmist, we can take our frustration, as well as those who may be the source of it, to God in prayer, trusting God to work toward a good and appropriate outcome for all. And we can be at peace, like the sun setting beautifully in the west at the close of day.

Psalm 8

Psalm 8 is one of the most beloved of the psalms. It celebrates and praises the Creator, the creation, and the astonishing gift of God's grace to human beings whom the psalm describes as God's very significant helpmates in manifesting God's kingdom on earth.

The good news, of course, is that in a creation as intricate, complex, and beautifully spun as the one of which we have been made a part, God holds a special regard for human beings. Yet, part of the esteem in which God holds human beings involves God entrusting extraordinary responsibility to us. One almost can hear the incredulity in the psalmist's voice when he exclaims to the Creator, *"You have given mortals dominion over the works of your hands?!"* Wow!

One of the greatest collective misunderstandings the human race ever has perpetrated on the planet is its erroneous perception of the word "dominion." What makes it even worse is that it has been a willful misinterpretation designed to feather our pockets and to choose convenience over conservation and profiteering over preservation. We have decided for our own benefit that "dominion" means domination, the result being that we now are encountering the calamitous effects of climate change, global warming, environmental degradation, and species extinction that affect all aspects of our public and personal lives, as well as the planet itself. We have cultivated a world order with a "scarcity mindset" as a rationale for setting ourselves against one another and the creation itself in our attempts to "secure security" for ourselves.

Dominion in the sense the psalmist uses it implies stewardship, friendship, servanthood, and safekeeping. Human beings are to be compassionate caretakers of all that God has made and entrusted to us. Moreover, human beings are those designated by God to bring forth "civilization" on earth, a holy kin-dom that works together for good for *all* in a way that honors God and tends God's creation. It is clear God believes we are up to it, with God's help, or "dominion" never would have been assigned to us in the first place.

We are to be midwives of a just and harmonious civilization in which dignity and respect are conferred on everyone everywhere and in which we *"love our neighbors as ourselves,"* as well as the whole of creation.

"O Lord, our Sovereign, how majestic is your name in all the earth!" May we, who live in the grace and goodness of that name, reflect that sublime majesty!

Psalm 9

Before God cares for each of us, God cares for all of us. That is a primary component not only of divine justice but also of the Divine Heart.

Why should particular peoples suffer because of their race, religion, nationality, gender identity or expression, sexual orientation, or geographic location? Why should life be stacked against children of poverty while their counterparts in families of means enjoy a surfeit of opportunities from which to choose and be advantaged?

While the idea of God as a personal chaplain may hold some appeal, especially to privileged people, our psalmist makes it clear that God is first and foremost a God of justice. *"The needy shall not always be forgotten, nor the hope of the poor perish forever."* We have a responsibility, not *for*, but *to*, those who are poor or hungry, relegated to outsider status, or otherwise denigrated and marginalized in our society. Only when it is well for all can it finally be well for each one. The psalmist is, in effect, saying that people's faith in God is for the benefit of others and not themselves only.

"God judges the world with righteousness," the psalmist affirms, *"and the peoples with equity."*

The purpose of God's judgment is not so much the punishment of sinners but the renovation of societies so that all may share in the grace, provision, and joy of God. Thus, the reign of God is inherently political, though not partisan, as politics is the public arena in which decisions are made that affect all peoples' lives. Nations, if they are so fortunate as to be able to choose their leaders, must choose wisely. Nations, if they are to flourish in God's reign, must care well for their people as well as the "strangers and foreigners" who come to them in want and hope, especially those who are oppressed or distressed both personally and systemically. *"Those who know your name, O God, put their trust in you."*

Those who resist such a reconciliation to righteousness may find the fruits of God's judgment difficult. But those who come home to the love harbored in the goodness of God will find life richer, deeper, and broader than ever they have known or imagined!

Psalm 10

Prayer is not held in high esteem in some quarters these days. I have noticed in recent years that in response to persons promising to offer their "thoughts and prayers" in sad or sinister situations, someone is quick to say grumpily, "We need more than thoughts and prayers." Okay, yes, sure, but prayer is essential. Prayer is a primary way of opening ourselves to the presence of God wherein we are given to see the just and righteous ways of God. Prayer is how we are sensitized to see better the human and planetary needs around us and the ways God empowers us to respond in God's name and purpose. Prayer is a way we yield to God and open ourselves to God's wisdom. Prayer is a way God can direct our actions. Prayer is a principal way God conveys God's promised grace and peace even in the most calamitous of circumstances. To say it succinctly, *prayer is being with God.* Thus, we can indeed, as Paul enjoins us to do, "pray without ceasing."

In Psalm 10, the psalmist inquires insistently of God why those who do not give two hoots about the plight of anyone but themselves often seem to prosper in life while those who are downtrodden or attempt to "keep the faith" sometimes feel bereft of God's presence and care.

But, then, in prayer, this psalmist also exclaims excitedly, *"Oh, God, you do see! Indeed, you note trouble and grief that you may take it into your own hands."*

The life of faith is not intended to be "Easy Street." God is no guarantor of an "express lane life" in which we simply breeze by others on our way to unrelenting comfort and success. There is something most profound in a life that acknowledges God sincerely and does not just talk about praying, but prays. We meet God in prayer and are brought into a consciousness of the deeper things of God and life. We find our contentment in the humility of serving God by loving our neighbors and the greater community. In that way, our neighbors' prayers often are answered, too.

Thoughts and prayers? By all means, for they serve as a gateway into our living toward and into the Beloved Community of God!

Psalm 11

The psalmist has decided to stake his life on God. *"In the Lord I take refuge,"* he states at the outset of the psalm. The psalmist was more than a little put out and put off when someone suggested in a difficult situation that he cut and run, abandon his commitment to God and neighbors, and do what was expedient for himself.

With so much tumult in our country today, and often in our own lives, we find ourselves tempted to take matters into our own hands and either give into despair or retreat into watching out for our own good only. Instead, we are counseled by the psalmist to heed God's continual call to care for the common good and the well-being of the larger communities of which we are a part. In so doing, we shall find ourselves being cared for as well.

"Take refuge in the Lord," indeed! It takes courage, commitment, humility, and faithfulness to entrust one's life to God in all seasons and circumstances of life and to live accordingly instead of trying to take all matters into our own hands. But, in the power of the Spirit of God, we can live together toward the hope and fruition of God's Beloved Community that is both already here (in acts of compassion, kindness, justice, love, and beauty) and yet to come in all of its glorious fullness!

Psalm 12

Not many people these days would argue with this psalmist's description of humanity. So many people lie to each other, he said. Our leaders lie. They obfuscate. They say anything to work circumstances and conditions to their own advantage. People say one thing to one person and something different to another. *"With a double heart they speak,"* the psalmist laments. "Whatever serves my purposes," is their inner mantra.

When leadership lowers the bar morally and ethically whether in church, country, factory, school, or family, a whole society begins to weaken. That is what the psalmist meant when he sang ruefully, *"The faithful have disappeared from humankind."* The psalmist is despondent and prays, *"May the Lord cut off all flattering lips and those who say, 'With our tongues, we will prevail; our lips are our own - who is our master?'"*

The "lies" that nations permit and promote are particularly heinous to God. When history is revised to deflect or rationalize the racism, genocide, fascism, authoritarianism, and inequality institutionalized in government actions, programs, and policies, and to justify the perpetuation of such, God is not pleased. God is not having it. *"Because the poor are in despair and the needy groan, I will rise up and act."* It is not the vain, empty falsehoods in which governments traffic that will win the day or their morally bankrupt acts, but the purposes and actions of God accomplished through God's divinely-empowered and faithful people. God does not have a double heart. *"The Lord's promises are pure,"* the psalmist affirms. *"They are like silver refined in a furnace."*

Our own false speaking is no less offensive and hurtful. As we read later in the New Testament, *"Let your yes be yes and your no be no."* Truthfulness is one of the primary bedrocks of relationships, communities, and lives that flourish.

Lies, deceit, and duplicity are their own traps into which liars, prevaricators, and duplicitous people eventually fall and fail. Far better to speak and to do the truth after God's own manner and means!

Psalm 13

No human being is exempt from the vagaries and vicissitudes of life. Faith is not a talisman against what the hymn writer calls "dangers, toils, and snares." We find we must endure stretches when hardly anything seems to go right for us or when we feel broken down spiritually, emotionally, and/or physically, or when it seems as if everything and everyone are against us. Psalm 13 is a prayer for such times. Notice the honesty with which the psalmist prays that is commensurate with his feelings and assessment of his current life situation.

"How long, O Lord? Will you forget me forever? How long will you hide your face from me? How long must I bear pain in my soul and sorrow in my heart all day long?"

Of course, God never forgets us nor hides from us nor inflicts pain on us. It may feel that way because of our mistaken presumption that faith should spare us hardships and hard news. It helps me to remember that even Jesus suffered profoundly.

In the end, the psalmist realizes we do not normally get precise answers to questions like "How long?" We do not get timetables or details about when or how relief will come. But we do get God! Nothing can be better than "God with us" in all times and circumstances!

"I trusted in your steadfast love, O God; my heart shall rejoice in your salvation. I will sing to the Lord, because God has dealt bountifully with me."

Always! Even when it seems otherwise, God is working God's good purpose out in us and for us. As the late Jim Valvano, then the coach of North Carolina State's men's basketball team famously said in his valedictory, "Don't give up. Don't ever give up."

Psalm 14

The atheists about whom this psalmist is praying are those who claim with their mouth to believe in God but who deny God in their hearts and actions, who install themselves as the center of their lives, who fashion a god in their own image. Indeed, in their minds they essentially make themselves their own god.

These people do so because the true God is an inconvenience as they pursue their own unrighteous plans and power and do not want any "holy" or "righteous" interference. They want to be *the* Authority Figure in their lives. They want to accrue power to themselves. They want to make themselves "big" by belittling others. They crave control and, since they cannot control Divine Mystery, they discount and deny it altogether. They convince themselves they are free to live according to their own dictates and desires. They have no idea of what is meant by serving others. They expect only for their own whims to be served.

The psalmist calls these people "fools." To disbelieve in the Creator God, revealed fully in Jesus Christ, finally is foolhardy. But God remains open and favorably disposed to all of us. If and when those who say there is no God, or who make in their minds a god that enables their own base instincts, respond to the One always knocking on the door of their hearts, they, too, will come to meet and experience the God of steadfast love, mercy, and joy. Then, their lives (*our* lives?) will be transformed toward the good of all.

So may it be!

Psalm 15

Like sunlight breaking through clouds to make a river shimmer and shine, so does Psalm 15 illuminate our lives with the light of God.

According to Jewish tradition, the Torah contains 613 commandments from the Lord, the most familiar of which are the "Ten Commandments." The author of this psalm, identified by the editors of the psalter to be King David, summarized the 613 commandments into those expressed in this psalm.

They provide the moral and ethical spine of a life worth living and pleasing to God, the bones with which the kingdom of God and the Beloved Community rise up in our midst as we add our flesh and blood to them. We later hear their echoes all through the gospel of Jesus Christ with his double-command summary: *"Love the Lord your God with all your heart and with all your soul and with all your mind. And love your neighbor as yourself."* (And, by the way, that command does not mean to love our neighbors *as much as* ourselves but to love our neighbors, to treat our neighbors, as if indeed they *are* us.) In other words, stop "othering" others. We *all* belong to one family, God's family!

But it all begins in this psalm that serves as prelude and underpinning to that double-command: *"Speak the truth; do not slander; stay true to your word; do no evil; do no harm; do not accuse falsely; keep your promises; refuse to participate in wickedness; care for those who assume risks to honor God in all circumstances; do not profit at others' expense; do not conspire against the innocent."*

We do not keep the Lord's commandments in order to earn God's love, but because we are loved by God already. We do not live the life Psalm 15 describes without God's help, without God stirring this radical newness in us. So, with full confidence in the largesse of God's love, in its complete sufficiency and efficacy for our lives, we indeed may live lovingly by God's grace and generosity. Not only shall we ourselves benefit but also all others with whom we have to do.

Then, too, as the psalmist testifies, we shall not blow hot and cold nor to and fro on the winds of culture. Instead, we shall become steady and steadfast in the ways of God that make for faithful, gracious, and generous living.

Psalm 16

Choosing to come to God for what God can do for us is understandable. But choosing to come to God in love, reverence, gratitude, and hope because God is God is of a higher order.

The former allows us (mistakenly) to think of God as a servant to our "asks" and wants. We get angry or disillusioned if God does not meet our demands and desires. It can lead to our falling away from faith because we think our prayers have not been answered (or that the Cosmic Vending Machine didn't deliver, to put it more crassly), so why bother with God at all? Why? Because God joins us to "a goodly heritage" of all that God ever has done, is doing, and ever will do.

It is not for any particular outcome that we honor God with our worship and prayers but because God is God and is rightly to be praised. Trusting that *"we live and move and have our being in God"* (Acts 17:28) is enough. More than enough! What a gift! Trusting that we are beloved of God and in God's eternal care no matter what comes our way in this life is the most appropriate and fulfilling manner of responding to God. It is also the way of peace. It is true joy!

Trusting that God means well for us is a blessed assurance. The late Madeleine L'Engle, the author of *A Wrinkle in Time* and many other books, once wrote, "I have a point of view. You have a point of view. But God has view." We do not always know what is best for ourselves in the long run in the way that God does. So, frankly, sometimes we are better off if God does not honor our desires.

Psalm 16 sometimes is called the "golden Psalm." Others call it "David's Jewel." Why? Because it says beautifully and succinctly what is essential for us to do if our relationship with God is to grow and deepen. Love God for God's own sake. Trust and keep the faith that God finally will do what is best for us and in accord with God's perfect and eternal plan.

Psalm 17

Psalm 17 is a prayer expressing wariness and weariness over those who press a false narrative about us and will not let go of it.

"Guard me, God, as the apple of the eye; hide me in the shadows of your wings from those who are treacherous toward me and want to bring me down...who with their mouths speak arrogantly to me or about me."

Almost all of us have experienced people in our lives who unfairly have it out for us. Many times it is because we stand in the way of their desired version or vision of reality, their misplaced alignments, their own delusions bent to serve or to justify their own needs and purposes, a festering hurt inside of them, or simply because they are jealous of us.

These persons may think they know us but substitute their assumptions for real knowledge. They ascribe scurrilous motivations to us without ever talking with us about their concerns even when our track record lends their accusations no support. They manufacture conspiracy theories when there are no conspiracies.

There often is no convincing these "adversaries" they are misguided and on the wrong track. It becomes counterproductive to continue to try to do so. So, what do we do?

Look to God and not to those who falsely accuse, says the psalmist. Though difficult to do, it is the best way for us to be freed from the tyranny of their trying and troubling ways.

Entrust the sorry situation and those who are the cause of it to God, and then let us move on with our lives in trust and hope.

Psalm 18

This psalm is a veritable collection of affirmations of God by David after God had delivered David out of the grip and grasp of enemies and adversaries. *"I love you, O Lord, my strength. The Lord is my rock, my fortress, my deliverer; my God, my rock in whom I take refuge, my shield, and the horn of my salvation, my stronghold."*

Do we similarly acclaim and cry out in glad and grateful exclamations when God has delivered us from danger, desolation, or despair? Do we praise God as first-order business when we have been brought safely through a tight spot in our lives? *"You gave me a wide place for my steps under me,"* David the psalmist exclaims to God. *"You brought me out into a broad place,"* into the spaciousness of God's salvation.

David recounts what happened when his situation became desperate. *"In my distress I cried to my God for help and God heard my voice; my cry reached God's ears."* Then, God acted. Using metaphor in verses 7-15, David describes the momentous and crucial help God provided to him. David then spends much of the rest of this psalm-prayer lifting up the goodness of God.

"It is you, God, who lights my lamp, who lights up my darkness."

"This God - God's way is perfect."

David is empowered now. He no longer feels as though he only can plod and lumber along through life. With God's presence and help, he can *"leap over a wall."* Not just a religious idea or principle, God is God! God is a God who acts, who is real, who is committed to God's people. Awed by what God can do, David fairly sings, *"The Lord lives! Blessed be my rock and exalted be the God of my salvation!"*

Psalm 19

I have cherished this psalm for a long time, and not only because it opens with its testimony that the creation itself is a witness to the grandeur of God. There are other psalms that do that. I am exuberant about Psalm 19 because it counters the critique of those who do not really know God, those who insist that God is a stick-in-the-mud and that God's intent is to suck all of the pleasure out of life. These sideline critics know just enough about God to get God all wrong.

The "laws and precepts" of God are not for the purpose of making our lives smaller or more constricted. They are for the purpose of opening us to the fullness of human life that only is possible when we are living toward the Beloved Community...when doing justice, loving kindness, walking humbly, and making the world more tender are our priorities...when caring for society's "last, lost, least, and littlest" is more of a primary desire than building bigger and bigger barns (modern translation: portfolios) to hoard our own treasure and to serve ourselves.

There is a reason Psalm 19 says the precepts and ordinances of the Lord *"are more to be desired than gold, even much fine gold"* and that they are *"sweeter than honey and drippings of the honeycomb."* It is because those precepts and ordinances are true. It is because they show us *"the still more excellent way."* We can count on their reliable wisdom because God is behind them. It is because they encourage us not to be seduced by the world's allures, temptations, and values. It is because they rescue us from living puny lives and carry us into the heart of life. Those who want to be opened to the splendor of their full humanity and to the glory of God will embrace them for, as this psalmist sings, *"The precepts of the Lord are right and rejoice the heart!"* They nurture our relationship with God that, in turn, transforms our relationships with others as well as the way we see and experience ourselves.

The psalm concludes with a heartfelt and earnest prayer that we are invited to make our own even as we join the rising crescendo of a great choir of people who have prayed it in every age: *"May the words of my mouth and the meditation of my heart be acceptable to you, O Lord, my rock and my redeemer."* Oh, yes!

Psalm 20

The psalms were, and often still are, *sung* in the setting of public worship. Even when we read and pray them in personal devotion, we can imagine in our mind the vast array of Jewish and Christian congregations of people in which the psalms have been read, prayed, and set to music across many centuries. Even when we are alone, we are yet a part of the great chorus of God's people of every time and place.

That being said, Psalm 20 locates the liturgical leader in a worship service where the congregation is gathered in prayer for someone, likely a king of ancient Israel, involved in a conflict needing to be resolved. While praying for competence and compassion for our leaders charged with making decisions, the psalmist reminds the congregation that people of God do not put their trust in chariots, princes, war horses, or weapons, but in God and God's ways.

That's a heavy lift, isn't it? The "world" to this day too often puts its trust in wealth and might and power and fighting prowess. But doing it the world's way hasn't brokered any consistent or lasting peace. Perhaps that is why, in the Garden of Gethsemane when the authorities came to arrest Jesus and one of his followers used his sword to cut off the ear of a soldier, Jesus ordered his disciple to put it away, saying, *"All who take up the sword will die by the sword"* (Matthew 26:52).

Yet, even the people of God have been reluctant to lay down our arms - weapons of metal or words - and *"to take our pride in the name of the Lord our God."* Is it because we are not convinced that the wisdom and ways of God work in the "real world"? Do we believe they ultimately lack sufficient power?

Thank God, Jesus did not waver. Even when it became clear that following the divine prescription for life would lead to his death, Jesus remained steadfast in his commitment to

God. So also did God remain faithful to Jesus and raised him from death into life eternal. The resurrection of Jesus was, and is, a vindication of the ways of God in the world.

Salvation ultimately belongs to God and, therefore, *by God's grace and gift*, does it come to the children of God.

Psalm 21

I still am learning what this psalmist knew long ago. It usually is strategic for one's own mental, emotional, spiritual and, sometimes, physical well-being not to fight one's "enemies" but to release them to God. It is best to respond to others and their unfair and unjust behaviors toward us not according to who they are but according to who we are. When people oppose, undercut, or disrespect us, utter slander or evil against us falsely, or act out their enmity toward us, especially in cruel or devious ways, it is very hard to stem our desire to give them what we believe they are due, to hurt them even more than they have hurt us. Ultimately, though, that satisfies only momentarily because "payback" is not a part of our better nature and we know it.

We do not have to be pushovers, of course. When someone acts destructively or wantonly toward us, we can express and address ourselves appropriately to the one or ones offending against us and/or to proper authorities. But, then, give the person or persons over to God. We do not want to get into a "race to the bottom" with those who deal with us in unkind, unseemly, or unspeakable ways. The psalmist trusts God to deal with "enemies" according to God's own choosing. We can, too.

A thousand or so years after this psalm was written, St. Paul confirmed the psalmist's wisdom: *"Beloved, never avenge yourselves, but leave room for the reproof of God."* It still is wise counsel today. We are assured that our adversaries, as much as we ourselves, will be handled by God in a manner both just and redemptive. So, we can exclaim with the psalmist: *"Be exalted, O Lord, in your strength. We will sing and praise your power."*

Let us not try to outdo those who diminish themselves by their malign actions. Have our respectful say with them if we will or must, but then deliver them in prayer to God and let us get on with our life and witness to the "Light of the world." For God will accomplish God's purposes. In this psalm, the king confesses that his life and reign are from God and acknowledges that, apart from a relationship with God, he is only a wisp of what he otherwise could be.

The same is no less true of us.

Psalm 22

Psalm 22 reaffirms that our feelings and surmises are not reliable indicators of what God is doing in our lives. Even as Jesus cried aloud from the cross the opening words of this psalm - *"My God, my God, why have you forsaken me?"* - that wasn't his ultimate reality as the resurrection of Jesus dramatically reveals. God was with Jesus in his suffering as much as in his glory.

It is not that our feelings are "wrong." We feel what we feel. But our feelings can be misleading. They can be part of the story without being the whole story. Our emotions can be deceiving in regard to the truth of what actually is occurring in our lives and in terms of what God is doing in, through, and among us.

Memory is a better barometer of what God is doing in us than what we are experiencing existentially. Here is a general rule: "What God has done, God will do." As God has liberated, led, and loved God's people in the past, so God will continue to do again and again in our lives.

Pain is real. Suffering is real. But, as this psalm teaches, they are not ultimate. God has a track record. This psalm that began in deep despair ends in radiant hope and eternal praise. "Life" is always God's last word. Thanks be to God, always, forever!

Psalm 23

I think it is likely David wrote this psalm in the evening of his life. There is good scholarly warrant for such a conjecture even if no certainty, but I take comfort in picturing it so.

We best make sense of our lives in retrospect. Thus, I can imagine David in this psalm taking stock of his life – the good, the bad, and the hideous – and making Psalm 23 his prayer of gratitude at the end of it. David wants to share with his worshiping community and with God that which he has come to understand about his life as a result of his long relationship with God.

God was like a shepherd to David, even, especially, when David strayed. When crashing waves of immorality or immaturity threatened to undo him, God led David beside still waters to reflect and to change the direction of his life. When enemies crowded in around him, either internal or external, God offered guidance and a way through the dangerous morass. God restored David's soul whenever it was crushed in shame or sorrow. In the dark valleys of his life, David, with God's help, was able to tame his fear as he trusted that God's love never would let go of him. God was a calming companion to David and provided sustaining courage and encouragement whenever David was physically or spiritually lacking.

And then came David's final word of assurance – his certainty that whatever befell him in life, and at this life's end, he could count on the goodness and mercy of the Lord to attend him!

Psalm 24

For a long time in my life, Psalm 24 confounded me. After praising the sovereign God for creating the world and everything in it, the psalmist asks who will be able, who will be permitted, to keep company with the Lord of all.

The psalmist's response sets the bar so high it seems none, no one, no mortal, could qualify: *"Those who have clean hands and pure hearts..."* I don't have to think too long or hard to know I have neither, and any deeply honest person readily will admit the same. As hard as we may try, I, you, we, fall short of the glory of God.

Then one day it dawned on me that the psalmist is not describing how we see ourselves but how God sees us. We qualify not on our own merits, metrics, or machinations but as recipients of *"the blessing and vindication of the God of our salvation."* It is not by luck or pluck that we are welcomed into God's embrace, but by God's love for us from our very beginning.

With jargon sounding a little strange to our modern ears, the last part of the psalm encourages us to accept God's acceptance of us: *"Lift up your heads, ye mighty gates!"* Live as people who know we are held high in God's heart. We show forth God's lavish love in our lives by doing justice, practicing generosity, and living with integrity. In other words, by loving our neighbors in every way, every day.

Psalm 25

With every passing year of my life; no, with every fleeting month and day, these words of the psalmist give expression more and more to my deepest heart:

"Make me to know your ways, O Lord; teach me your paths. Lead me in your truth, and teach me, for you are the God of my salvation."

Maybe it's that I am old enough now to have seen other ways and to have tried some of them. None of them hold the beauty, gravitas, grace, compassion, or joy of the ways of God. None of them offer the coherence or cohesiveness to my life that God's ways do. None of them move or turn my heart toward others and the kin-dom of God in like manner to the Lord's ways. All other ways ultimately prove futile or unsatisfying.

"All the paths of the Lord are steadfast love and faithfulness..." the psalmist sings. Though they lead to a joyful end, God's paths are not undemanding. Committing ourselves to God's ways means involving ourselves compassionately in our neighbors' lives, seeking justice and dignity for those to whom they too long have been denied, and looking after the interests of others in need of help, healing, or hope. It is a full plate in the midst of also taking care of ourselves and those for whom we bear some direct responsibility. But in doing so we experience *"the friendship of the Lord,"* as the psalmist calls it, an experience like no other. For even when we fall short of God's desire for us or even of our own expectations,

the Lord will lift us up. *"Do not remember my transgressions, Lord, but in your steadfast love, remember me."* God does exactly that and we experience God's redeeming grace as more and more we commit ourselves to the holy friendship God offers us.

"O my God, in you I trust." Yes! Amid all that is happening in the world and in our own lives, and even in full view of our sin and repeated failures, trusting in the One who loves us most of all and *whose love knows no end* really does make all the difference between a life lived in doubt and fear and one lived in hope and joy.

Psalm 26

Have you ever had to make a case for yourself? Or, perhaps, you have had to defend yourself in an instance when you thought you had been accused or judged unfairly?

That is how I read this psalm...the psalmist is polishing his dossier that God will "read" before passing judgment on him. The psalmist presents himself in the best possible light - *"I have trusted in the Lord without wavering"..."I wash my hands in innocence"..."I hate the company of evildoers, and I will not sit with the wicked"...*

To the psalmist's credit, he does go on to invite, perhaps even to implore, the Lord to "check under the hood" of his life, to be sure that his claims comport with reality, that he indeed is living in the way he claims to be living.

Perhaps, deep down, the psalmist fears God's judgment. What the psalmist must come to know in his heart is that God's judgment is never for the purpose of condemning us but restoring us, not punishing us but instructing us, not banishing or abandoning us but welcoming us and abiding with us always in love and hope. The father in the gospel parable of the prodigal son (Luke 15:11-32) betokens the largesse and love of God for us. No one is beyond the repair and redemption of God!

While God-followers are not finally to eschew or shun those who do not walk in integrity or who disbelieve in God or do not follow in God's ways, nevertheless, the psalmist also knows he needs the company of other believers, the friendship of those who delight in the Lord. Twice the psalmist intimates the necessity for a congregation of people with whom he can worship and walk in the strength and encouragement of God.

Indeed, while the psalms can be prayed by individuals, they come out of a worshiping congregation and thus are communal prayers in their origin. In reality, even when we pray the psalms in solitude, we are praying with a great congregation of people past and present.

Oh, yes! Behold the grace and grandeur of God! May we accept them as the gifts they are and then live our gratitude in the everydayness of our lives!

Psalm 27

A few years ago I made a paper copy of Psalm 27, rolled it up into a little scroll, and placed it in a crevice in the bark of a tree on one of my morning walking trails. I meant it as a gift for some future walker who would happen by, see it, and be curious enough to take and read it. The next time I passed by that tree, about a week later, my little psalm gift was gone. I like to think it was not a squirrel who found it but a person who needed to read exactly this psalm at that particular time.

Psalm 27 is a life-changing psalm if we will trust its message. The first verse well captures its essence with the remainder of the psalm being variations on this very consequential theme:

"The Lord is my light and salvation; whom shall I fear? The Lord is the stronghold of my life; of whom shall I be afraid?"

External enemies and internal demons can make life miserable or confounding at times, but we belong to God. *"Though an army encamp against me, my heart shall not fear; though war rise up within me, yet will I be confident."*

Where is your life rooted? In present situations and circumstances? In your own abilities? In your reputation and popularity? If so, the odds are that you will be blown "to and fro" and "here and there" on the many and various winds of change and happenstance. But if, like this psalmist, you ask one thing of God - *"to live in the household of the Lord all the days of my life"* - your heart will be encouraged to believe and to live in the goodness of God your stronghold, always, come what may. And from that vantage point, you can *"do justice, love kindness, and walk humbly with God."*

This psalm speaks to the depth of human need and the height of God's love! Let that love hold you and lift you up, and then send you forth, all of your days.

Psalm 28

Psalm 28 contains a call for divine vengeance against both the psalmist's enemies as well as those whom the psalmist regards as enemies of God. It's a call that later was to be radically transformed by Jesus' admonition to love and to pray for one's enemies. Still, I appreciate Psalm 28 for this important reminder it contains:

"Blessed be the Lord who has heard the sound of my pleadings...so I am helped, and my heart exalts, and with my song-prayer, I give thanks to God."

"So, I am helped..." God always answers our prayers, sometimes in obvious ways, other times in ways more obscure, and in still other instances in ways we may not immediately understand or appreciate. But since one of the deepest truths about God is that God always means well for us, we can trust that God works everything in our lives for eventual and ultimate good as we live into God's purpose for life and our lives.

Are we thankful to God only when God's "answers" to our prayers are to our liking and meet with our immediate approval? Or, trusting God's grace, can we say to our Lord, even when the divine answer seems to be at odds with our own wisdom or desire, *"I believe; help Thou mine unbelief"*? And, *"Not my will, but Thy will be done, O God"*?

Trusting that God is who God claims to be and does what God promises to do is the heartbeat of our life and faith. The old saw applies: "Let go and let God." Let God fill our lives with grace and peace instead of constantly grappling with the strife that inevitably occurs when we try to retain ultimate control of our lives.

Psalm 29

Whether it's the *"still, small voice"* the prophet Elijah "heard" or the thundering voice that *"causes the oaks to whirl and strips the forest bare,"* people of faith listen to and for the voice of God in its many expressions.

God's voice isn't usually audible, though, indeed, God can speak to us through other people. God's voice often is an inner voice, an inner knowing, that "speaks" authoritatively to us through God's Spirit. It is a message, a consciousness, or a call that can come quietly or in more dramatic, thunderous, ways. It is a voice that echoes the gospel Jesus came preaching, teaching, and living. The voice of God never, ever, will ask us to believe or to do anything that does not comport with the teaching and spirit of Jesus.

Importantly for our days, empire is not God; only God is God.

The voice of God also has the power (the metaphorical "thundering" in this psalm) to guide, disturb, transform, and to heal our lives. Thus, prayer is at least as much, and usually more, about listening and discerning than speaking. When we turn a deaf ear to God, when we do not make a priority of listening to our lives, life begins to diminish spiritually and then, eventually, in every other way. The late poet, Mary Oliver, says in her poem, *"Praying,"* that prayer "is the doorway into thanks, and a silence in which another voice may speak."

It takes intention, attention, and practice to become adept at hearing the voice of the Lord in our lives, but no special skill. Stay alert, awake, and aware, and begin each day by praying, "Speak, Lord, for I am listening."

And may we, each and all of us, cry, "Glory!"

Psalm 30

It is not always, or even usually, an improvement in our circumstances that makes life qualitatively better for us. It may seem that way, of course. It did for this psalmist who had been healed from a severe illness. Most of us are happier in plenty than in want, in health than in sickness.

But, when we are dependent on favorable conditions or outcomes for our contentment, life can change in an instant via a sudden market crash, the death of someone close to us, the loss of a job, the treachery of a friend, a serious illness, or any of many other sobering life events.

It was St. Augustine who famously wrote that "our hearts are restless until they find their rest in God" and Psalm 30 seconds that motion. It is not finally the good fortune that may attend us that leads us into joy. It is the deep-seated knowledge that our God is Emmanuel - God with us - no matter the season or situation of our lives. It often is, in fact, the more difficult storylines in our lives by which we are led deeper into God.

It is as we truly open ourselves to God that we experience the Lord *"turning our mourning into gladness and our sackcloth into a garment of joy."* When the psalmist exclaims that *"weeping may tarry for the night but joy comes in the morning,"* he was speaking poetically, metaphorically. Relief from desperation and the turn to transformation does not always, even usually, happen immediately, but it does happen surely and certainly. My middle daughter, Katy, died over two decades ago at the age of eighteen and, though I still carry shards of grief in my heart, my weeping has been overcome by trusting God's promise that Katy has been swept up, too, in the glorious resurrection of Christ.

Buoyed by God's assurances, we may trust that a new morning always will come and, with it, an abundant measure of God's gladness.

Psalm 31

I find verse 14 of Psalm 31 to be, embarrassingly enough, a great challenge! Easy to read; harder to implement.

"But I trust in you, O Lord; I say, 'You are my God.'"

It is no problem for me to trust God theoretically, hypothetically, or in the printed Sunday liturgies of worship. But trusting God existentially and personally in my daily life is another matter altogether. If I am ruthlessly honest, trusting in myself, in my own intellect and abilities, seems too often to be my default orientation. The song I too often sing is not "God is working God's purposes out" but "Tom is (trying to) work Tom's purposes out." It is wearying to be, essentially, my own god. I have neither the qualifications, power, persistence, nor wisdom to fill the position.

In my better moments, I know that if only what can be proved by logic, reason, or in a laboratory is worthy of our belief and devotion, then life would be quite small indeed. But nothing is impossible with God. Mystery is that which prevents us from reducing life to a size and dimension we can manage and control. Mystery affirms that life and God always are more than we can ask, think, or imagine!

Faith itself is a mystery, but always a good one, as faith is a gift of God. Faith is not given to us as a way of figuring everything out. Faith is given to us as a relationship with the One *"in whom we live and move and have our being."* That is why any talk about "wanting more faith" or "needing more faith" misses the mark. Faith, for Christians, is a relationship with God in Christ through the power of the Holy Spirit. Thus, we always have more-than-sufficient faith available to us because God promises to be with us always. The "one thing needful" for faith to flower in us is to pay attention to our relationship with God in Christ.

The psalmist makes it clear that we will not know the peace of God in all of the circumstances of our lives until we trust God. Trusting that God is mysteriously but surely present in every aspect and instant of our lives, and working for our good in the context of the common good of all, enables us to live into the fullness of our faith. Praying scripture's psalms that witness to God's faithfulness, and thus immersing ourselves in the grace-filled milieu of God, is one way of helping us to do so.

While sin, self-centeredness, and hubris constrict our lives, making them smaller than we were created to be, this psalmist describes God's mercy and forgiveness as *"setting our feet in a broad place."* God's salvation feels like spaciousness, like we have room to breathe and thus to live into our true and full humanity. Thanks be to God!

Psalm 32

How hard it can be to admit our sin! But when we don't, when we carry it within us, if we have any conscience at all, unconfessed sin becomes like a sharp pebble in our shoe from which there is no relief. At least not until we get it out. Likewise, our soul blisters and festers within us until we confess it.

When we think we can hide, forget, or stash our sin out of sight and mind, we delude ourselves. We can try to bury it, but it will keep rising to the surface of our lives in a variety of unsavory ways. You undoubtedly have heard the expression, "Confession is good for the soul." It is more than that. This psalmist is telling us it is imperative for strong and healthy spiritual and emotional lives. Researchers also have documented, and our own experience confirms, that we suffer physically from the effects of carrying unrelieved sin in our lives.

There are few things in life more liberating and freeing than the feeling that accompanies the act of confession and receiving and accepting forgiveness. Until we confess our sin we remain constricted and constrained, and peace eludes us. As God invites our confession, God is faithful in forgiving.

"Then I acknowledged my sin to you, O God, and I did not hide my iniquity. I said, 'I will confess my transgressions to the Lord,' and you forgave the guilt of my sin." Thanks be to God!

When we are able to address our transgression with the person or persons against whom we have sinned, it often is good to do so. When we cannot, one's prayer ought also to include a plea to God to heal the hurt we may have caused in someone's life. Social sins in which we are complicit require not only confession but, as a response, a personal commitment to living and acting justly.

Remembering that sin can be both personal and communal, a question emerges for each of us: Do I have any unconfessed sin from which I need to be unburdened?

Psalm 33

Nations are not meant to usurp the place of God, the psalmist insists. Empires, nations, and governments are not intended to be our masters or overlords but the political and social means by which the revealed heart of God can be given tangible expression and encouraged. *"Happy is the nation"* this psalmist declares, *"whose God is the Lord."*

Nations are not meant to be sectarian religious entities, of course, nor theocracies, and they are not churches. But they are to facilitate the application and implementation of justice for all in its many forms and layers so that *everyone* may have the opportunity to thrive. The blessed emergence of the Beloved Community with its deep and abiding concern for neighbor love is to be supported and celebrated by the nations so that each and all may flourish.

Nations are to be non-violent in their relations with other nations. Psalm 33:16-17,20: *"A king is not saved by his great army...the war horse is a vain hope for victory and by its great might cannot save...Our soul waits for the Lord who is our help and shield."*

The Old Testament prophets warned ancient Israel it could not long stand if the hungry were not fed, widows and orphans were not attended, strangers and foreigners were not welcomed, the dignity of each person was not honored, those without means were not lifted up, and justice for each and all went missing. In every age, God is not mocked. A country's leaders and its people can learn a lot and avoid calamity and catastrophe by heeding the biblical prophets and taking the psalms to heart.

"Our heart is glad in God because we trust in God's holy name. Let your steadfast love, O Lord, be upon us, even as we hope in you." This is as true for nations as it is for individuals.

Psalm 34

No doubt you have been around a person or persons who are parsimonious with their praise, stingy. Perhaps it was, or is, a parent, maybe a spouse, possibly a colleague, boss, teacher, or friend. Maybe you see that penury in yourself. All share one characteristic: they lack humility.

It requires humility to praise another person, to put someone else's feelings, accomplishments, or betterment ahead of our own, to make others look good, to give someone else credit, and to draw attention away from ourselves to the person(s) we are praising. But it is a primary and essential Christian attribute. If, as St. Paul writes in Philippians 2, *"Jesus did not count equality with God as something to be exploited but humbled himself and took on human form..."* how can *we* faithfully aspire to anything but humility?

When our hubris crowds out our humility, we have lost our way. Our psalmist says, *"My soul makes its boast in the Lord; let the humble hear and be glad. O magnify the Lord with me, and let us exalt his name together."*

As this psalmist intimates, we owe everything to the Lord. Thus, our lives can be filled with thanks and praise to God without fear of being diminished ourselves in any way. All of our boasting, unless it finally is of God, is misplaced. It is God who enables and ennobles our lives.

Discover how your life changes when you become more profuse in your praise of God and then, too, in your praise of others. It is the best path I know to the glorious life of humility and joy.

Indeed, as the psalmist says, *"Look to God, and be radiant."*

Psalm 35

Speaking to the Lord, this psalmist prays, *"Say to my soul, 'I am your salvation.'"*

For some, "salvation" is an awkward word. Part of the reticence, unfortunately, may be pride, as in, "I don't need to be saved. I am doing fine on my own." Others belittle the word by insisting that salvation narrowly means the saving of our souls by Jesus for heaven. Salvation becomes the ticket out of this life into the next one.

But salvation has a larger meaning and it is, I believe, the one intended by the psalmists. In this understanding, salvation is first of all for this life, this world. We are saved by God's grace from immersing ourselves in the values, prizes, and siren songs of the world's ways and arrogance that lead us astray from living graciously. We are saved from living egotistical, selfish, lives. We are saved, instead, to participate in the reign and realm of God, the kingdom and kin-dom of God, in the midst of this world that God loves. The salvation life is the leaven God uses to make the whole world to rise into a Beloved Community of compassion, justice, hospitality, generosity, and joy.

We are saved from a life in which we install ourselves at the center of it, serve only and primarily our own needs and desires, and too often get caught up in pettiness. We are saved *for* a life much larger in which we are alive from God the Center, serve our neighbors in need of liberation, opportunity and compassion, and pray for those who sin against us.

Indeed, God, please say again and again to my soul, *"I am your salvation."* Present tense. Betokened by our baptism, salvation is not only for a life to come but for this now and present life.

Psalm 36

Psalm 36 needs to be heard loud, clear, and often in our world. After running through a litany of characteristics of those who live and work against God's purposes (the worst offenders, in both the psalmist's and my own opinions, are *"those who flatter themselves in their own eyes,"* as hubris is the great destroyer of community and the common good), the psalmist gives a clarion endorsement of God's ways:

"How precious is your steadfast love, O God! All people may take refuge in the shadow of your wings...For with you is the fountain of life; in your light we see light."

It is true to my experience that we best see the faithful life we are called to live as we live it. *"In God's light we see light."* From the outside, it may be hard to imagine why we would look after the interests of others (Philippians 2:4) or forgive seventy times seven times (Matthew 18:22) or pray for those who persecute us (Matthew 5:44) or pay someone who only worked the last hour of the day the same wage as someone who has worked all day (Matthew 20:1-16).

But, from the inside, we can see more clearly what God is doing as well as the enlightened life God is working out in us and through us. There, life makes sense. Life coheres. Life grows more expansive. *"In God's light we see light."* We don't wait until we have it all figured out to entrust our lives to God. *"In God's light we see light."*

Come into God's light so you can see what God is doing, and then know the great joy of joining God in doing it!

Psalm 37

Psalm 37 is one I need to read, hear, and pray over and over again. In it, the psalmist repeatedly advises patience.

Spiritual patience is waiting on the Lord. In this case, waiting is not synonymous with doing nothing. Waiting on God, in a phrase philosopher Friedrich Nietzsche coined and Christian pastor and author Eugene Peterson later made famous, encourages "a long obedience in the same direction." Active waiting, for a Christian, means living faithfully in accord with God's ways that we can see clearly in Christ, trusting that God is working life toward God's good purposes all the while.

It means not wavering in the face of seemingly unrighteous people appearing to do well in life or unscrupulous people getting ahead or gaining power. Trusting that humility and love signaled by Christ's ministry and in Christ's gospel are of more import than self-aggrandizement and swagger, and of more significance than burnishing our own reputation, we do not take a detour from God's highway but stay steadfastly on that divine road.

We trust, as this psalmist several times affirms, that the ways of people that are not in keeping with God's ways will not finally stand. *They will fade like grass.* Patiently living a life congruent with God's heart, admittedly a challenge when those who do not do so often seem to prosper in power and riches by the world's accounting, nevertheless and without fail leads to deep and abiding joy.

Patience! Spiritual patience trusting that God is faithful to God's promises.

Psalm 38

Sin not only has moral and ethical consequences. Often, it also has physical dimensions. I know from experience how my sin sometimes has laid me low in grief, remorse, or shame and how I have felt it with "twisted insides" and a hurting heart.

This psalmist describes it like this:

"I am utterly bowed down and prostrate; all day long I go around mourning...I am utterly spent and crushed; I groan because of the tumult of my heart...my iniquities weigh on me like a burden too heavy."

Sin often *seems* attractive, exciting, adventurous, advantageous, or fulfilling. If it didn't, we wouldn't be so eager to engage it. Unable to *"wait on the Lord,"* we give into sin's seductive allure that, as our conscience works in us, we regret, sometimes immensely so, and to the point where our bodies bear the anguish:

"I am ready to fall, and my pain is ever with me. I confess my iniquity; I am sorry for my sin. Make haste to help me, O Lord, my salvation."

But, just then, by God's utter and amazing grace, we are helped by this same God upon whom we call. We are forgiven, made new, and set free to live holy, wholehearted, and joyful lives.

Psalm 39

Though it always is true, especially now that I am in the last third of my life, I find great resonance with this psalm:

"Lord, let me know my end, and what is the measure of my days; let me know how fleeting my life is...Surely everyone stands as a mere breath."

When I find pictures of classmates and friends on social media whom I have not seen in forty years, or look in the mirror and compare what I see there to a photograph from earlier in my life, I marvel at the aging process and how quickly life passes. Thus, like the psalmist, I want to live the time remaining to me in a manner respectful of, and responsible to, the ways and will of God. No matter our age, the earlier we learn that discipline the better it will be for us and for those around us.

"Keeping a muzzle on my mouth" is good counsel if I am only trying to win an argument with someone or to prove a point. There is enough division and conflict in the world and in our relationships without piling on my pettiness. However, if someone can be helped or served by my voice bearing witness to injustice, inhospitality, or inhumanity, or by hearing a word of kindness, I need to use it loudly and clearly.

Praying to God, this psalmist says, *"My hope, O Lord, is in you."* As life is flying by, this psalm tells me whose company I should be keeping and of whose wisdom I should be availing myself.

Psalm 40

Be sure to hold on to this gem from our Psalm 40 psalmist:

"Sacrifice and offering you do not desire, Lord, burnt offering and sin offering you have not required; but you have given me an open ear."

As I have indicated previously, one of the foremost lessons the psalms teach us is that a large part of prayer is listening. Let me say it again. A large part of prayer is listening. Likewise, a key part of reading scripture is to hear it as personal address. "Turn your eyes into ears" is how one of my mentors once described it to me.

God has given us an open ear so that we may listen to God's always-present Spirit before charging forth in our lives. It is one of the best ways we have for getting to know both God and ourselves. Our spiritual hearts have both eyes and ears open to perceiving the presence and leading of God.

It is true, as the Letter of James says, that *"faith without works is dead."* But it also is true what the psalmists say: *"Be still and know that I am God."* The latter is necessary in order to fuel the former lest we simply spin our wheels with busyness. What part does God want each of us to play in God's unfolding kin-dom, in God's Beloved Community? What does God have in mind for us at this present stage of our lives?

Here is how the esteemed American author, theologian, and civil rights leader Howard Thurman says it: "There is something in every one of you that waits and listens for the sound of the genuine in yourself…And if you cannot hear it, you will, all of your life, spend your days on the ends of strings that somebody else pulls." Wow!

God has given us an open ear. "Listen" for, and to, the word of the Lord!

Psalm 41

In this psalm, David recounts his own significant suffering caused by a combination of his own selfish sin, the treachery of friends, and, most distressing, treason within his own family. He is not at all happy. *"Even my bosom friend in whom I trusted, who ate of my bread, has lifted his heel against me."*

The psalmist reflects on the sublime reality that God has been more faithful to him than his human friends. Thus, David appeals to the Lord for continuing grace and help. One of the surprising things the psalmist "hears" from God in response is that even in the midst of his own pain and suffering, the psalmist is to provide succor for those who are vulnerable and at risk of sinking rather than swimming in life.

That is a bit of a wake-up call for me that at first seems counterintuitive. When I am in the slough of despond, either by my own cause or by the ill-manner of others, I am to eschew excessive wallowing and ramp up my heeding the just and gracious ways of God, and then doing them unto others.

When life turns sour for us, that's just the time when we are to help to make life better for others, for God is faithful to sustain us. Helping to improve the lives of others to whom we offer genuine and heartfelt care and compassion is a simultaneous pathway as well to our own healing. Indeed, "God works in mysterious ways, God's wonders to perform!"

Nowhere have I found words more powerful than those in the Psalms. Their fervid poetry cleanses one, gives one strength, brings hope in moments of darkness. Makes one look critically into oneself, convict oneself, and wash one's heart clean with one's own tears. It is the ever-burning fire of love, of gratitude, humility, and truth.

~Svetlana Alliluyeva

Psalm 42

God is not ancillary to our lives. God is the heart and center of our lives. God is not ephemeral. God is essential. This psalmist knows it:

"As a deer longs for flowing streams, so my soul longs for you, O God. My soul thirsts for God, for the living God."

It is fair to say that all true longing in this life is really a longing for God. Not an idea or concept of God, not an intellectualized version of God, but the real and very God *"in whom we live and move and have our being"* (Acts 17:28). Our longing for God may present as something else: a longing for love, for safety, or for well-being; a longing to belong; a longing to be understood or to understand; a longing to make a difference in another's life; a longing to be healed or held or cherished or forgiven. But, in the end, each of these longings is a flowering of our desire for God who encompasses all of those yearnings.

As the psalmist did, it helps us to confess our desire for God to abide in us as we abide in God. Let God be God. Let the psalmist's cry cited above become a part of our prayer life, too. Even in the difficult and dismaying times of our lives, even when God seems to be hidden or far away, especially then, continue to thirst for God. For then we shall find God's quenching, transforming grace flowing over, into, under, upon, and among us in ways we may never have imagined - always hopeful, many times challenging, and forever life-giving!

Psalm 43

Only five verses long, Psalm 43 nonetheless is a powerhouse.

Too often caught in a mental or emotional quagmire stemming from being treated unfairly, feeling unappreciated, or not being "seen," the psalmist prays for relief to the only One who finally can give it:

"Send out your light and your truth, O God; let them lead me." Let *them* lead me - God's light and God's truth - for they are part and parcel of God who is our help and refuge - not the naysayings or inattention of those from whom we had expected more recognition, compassion, friendship, or support.

There is a lot in life that drains us of energy and stamina. More times than we care to admit, we feel like folding up or into ourselves. But the psalmist commends a different response when our souls are cast down and our spirits are disquieted within us: *"Hope in God!"* Hope is not something we conjure up within us. True hope originates from beyond us, from the acts, actions, and presence of God bringing a fresh reality.

The psalmist encourages us to make a spiritual discipline of refusing to allow any emotional traps we encounter to ensnare us, hold us hostage, or, in contemporary parlance, to live rent-free in our heads. Rather, he tells us to hope unrelentingly in God for the light and love we need.

Then, by God's grace and in Christ Jesus, we shall find ourselves being delivered from our anguish.

Psalm 44

John Calvin, a leader in the Protestant Reformation and a pillar of the Reformed theological tradition, called the psalms "an anatomy of all parts of the soul." Every part of our soul and the full range of our emotions are given expression in the Psalms including, as in Psalm 44, the less elegant ones.

This psalmist is barking at God for being unresponsive to the needs and plights of the psalmist and his nation. He feels they are being debased and disgraced and that God isn't doing anything to help them. We have suffered through similar times of troubles and travails, haven't we, times when it has seemed as if God is absent, as if God is nowhere to be found, as if we have been abandoned, as if we are doing life alone?

How are we to respond when we feel like God's love has let go of us? What does the psalmist do? While being forthright about his feelings, he is wise enough to know that feelings can be deceptive and misleading. So he hangs onto the memories of how God has helped him and his people in the past and clings to his deep conviction that *God is doing so now even if it is not immediately apparent to him.* The psalmist trusts, believes, affirms, and acts on the premise and promise that God is faithful and nothing can separate us from God's love. From our vantage point, we see that indefatigable embrace most clearly in Jesus Christ.

God is faithful still, and always!

Psalm 45

At first blush, and maybe even second and third, it is hard exactly to know what to make of this psalm. There are scholarly nods in the direction of the psalm describing the wedding of a king. Alternately, some say it is a love song with poetic allusions to a developing sexual relationship. There is a resonant allure to such a romantic rendering of love so robust and deep.

Read from our perspective three thousand years later, though, the first part of the psalm through verse 9 often is seen by Christians as a prayer of praise and adoration to Jesus and a celebration of his ministry of equity, equality, equanimity, righteousness, and love.

The remainder of the psalm, then, is read as counsel for God-attuned people: we are to disentangle ourselves from conforming to the world and its ways so that we may live in the world as the "bride of Christ" and join Christ in giving expression to his gospel of love.

A married couple share all facets of their life together. In our wedding to God in Christ, we are privileged to share in the fullness of Christ's ministry in and to the world. A love song, indeed!

Psalm 46

"God is our refuge and strength, a very present help in trouble. Therefore, we will not fear..."

"God is in the midst of the city; it shall not be moved."

"The nations are in an uproar, the kingdoms totter; the Lord of hosts is with us."

"Be still and know that I am God."

There is something about reading and praying this psalm in stillness and quietude that makes God's presence palpable for me. Any fear in me begins to be assuaged and my anxiety mitigated. God is not far off or removed from humanity. Indeed, God lives in the midst of the city, which is to say that God dwells with mortals, with us, wherever we are. God is here. God is a *"very present help."*

In a time when nations all over the globe, including ours, are in tumult, turmoil, and great travail, it is a relief to be reminded that they, too, belong to God who will not forsake them or us. God is, indeed, a *"very present help."*

In our tempest-tossed lives, it is unspeakably refreshing and grace-filled to be invited to make a priority of taking time to stop, to be still, and to receive assurances of the mysteries, marvels, and never-failing fidelity of God. It is essential to be attentive to the mighty acts of God in history and to the movement of God in our own times. Only then can we be prepared adequately to live God-infused, God-faithful lives in the midst of our daily rounds of fear, hope, anxiety, busyness, despair, responsibilities, politics, and joy. Only then will God's gracious, wise, and life-giving Spirit flow unencumbered through us into the world as we meet it day by day.

Only then will we come to know that the surest thing about our lives is God.

Psalm 47

In this psalm, we are encouraged to voice our praise to God for what God has done. For, indeed, God "has the whole world in his hands."

Why sing songs of praise? Several times the psalmist answers, *"For God is the king of all the earth!"* For those not accustomed to language about kings and monarchies, there is a way to paraphrase the psalmist: *"God is sovereign over all the earth!"* Thus, hope abounds, for nothing is impossible with God, not even the healing and reconciliation of adversaries, enemies, and estranged friends. Nations, too!

That is good news that can help to calm our troubled hearts about the geo-political scenario of the world today. God is compassionate, just, and righteous. Ultimately, therefore, the world will embrace and take on these same peaceable attributes for the singular reason that this *is* God's world, the world that John 3:16 assures us God loves. What great purpose and meaning God bestows on us as God chooses to enlist our committed partnership and friendship in helping the Beloved Community to come to full flower in this world, this life!

Yes! *"Sing! Sing praise to God! Sing praise to God who is sovereign over all the earth!"* And then let us also live our praise in everything we do and are!

Psalm 48

"Great is the Lord and greatly to be praised in the city of our God...Walk about that city (Zion/Jerusalem), go all around it, count its towers, consider well its ramparts; go through its citadels, that you may tell the next generation that this is God, our God forever and ever. God will be our guide forever."

On one level, this is a psalm about Zion, about Jerusalem, known as the city of God, the city the Jews believed was the place of God's earthly habitation and thus the place from which the clarion claim of God's sovereignty was issued forth.

But on another deeper and intended level, Psalm 48 is encouragement and instruction for people of every age, including ours, to learn well the dimensions and distinctions of the metaphorical "city of God." We do well, by God's grace and our obedience, to acquire facility in the ways of God in the world that stand in deep contrast to the world's manner of operating. It is God who is our essential guide and it is God's ways that will lead us in the paths of right and righteous living. It is God who will bless us with the companionship of Christ in every concern and circumstance. It is God who *is the joy of all the earth.*

Yes! Indeed! Forever! *"Great is the Lord and greatly to be praised!"*

Psalm 49

Wow! This psalm is relentless! Over and over it declares how foolhardy and even worse it is to put our trust in wealth, riches, and material prizes.

Psalm 49 makes clear the real treasure in life is an open-heartedness toward God. There we find the grace of a call to holiness, to becoming and being our true selves.

That doesn't mean cultivating a prettified piety as we seemingly show our concern for the world or for our neighbors when in reality we are doing it mainly and mostly to make ourselves look good.

It means we are to nurture our God-infused soul in the midst of this life with its many temptations, one of the chiefest of which is being seduced by the faux promise of security that affluence appears, but only appears, to offer.

No amount of money can buy off death forever and no amount of wealth can purchase the abundant life that only a deepening relationship with God, including deepening relationships with those to whom God calls us, can yield.

Do I, do you, want to spend the rest of our lives becoming rich, or rich toward God? For anyone in doubt, Psalm 49 is your psalm!

Psalm 50

This psalm has provided great serenity and solace to me and to many others through the years. The first two verses of this psalm arguably are two of the most comforting in all of scripture:

"The mighty one, God the Lord, speaks and summons the earth from the rising of the sun to its setting. Out of Zion, the perfection of beauty, God shines forth!"

God initiates. We respond. God calls. We answer. We are prone to thinking we take the initiative in prayer. No! God invites us to pray and thus even our prayer is a response to God's prior offer of intimacy. The life in which we are set and the world into which we are sent are not our own doing but the creative handiwork of God. We do not begin anything. It all starts with God. God shines forth and we live and respond in God's luminous love.

St. Paul writes that *"God prepares good works for us beforehand that we should walk into them."* God creates opportunities. We avail ourselves of them, or not.

God always precedes us. There is no place we can go where God is not already present. Before we find God, God has found us. We do not earn or merit God's love and acceptance; rather, they are given to us by God as grace and gift at the outset of our lives and are confirmed for us in the rituals of Baptism and Holy Communion.

God initiates. God creates. God calls us to life. We respond with a *"sacrifice of thanksgiving"* in the words of this psalm. We answer with our lives of just, joyous, and willing obedience! In other words, true freedom!

Psalm 51

Psalm 51 is a prayer of confession suitable for every season and occasion of our lives.

The pathos of the sinner in the opening verses is heart-rending. If we are honest, though, we know he speaks also for us. The psalmist insists that, finally, all sin is sin against God for it breaks the unity, joy, wholeness, and peace God desires for God's creation. Sin disrupts relationships and undercuts justice.

Remorseful for his sin, the psalmist wants his life to be set straight, something he knows finally can happen only through the grace and friendship, the clemency and compassion, of God. *"Create in me a clean heart, O God, and put a new and right spirit within me...Restore to me the joy of your salvation."*

All of us have experienced the ways sin can mar and scar our personal lives. The same is true in our life together as church, community, and nation. Sin can bend us low but God's mercy, experienced as healing and forgiveness, can raise us high.

May each of us, sinners all, with broken and contrite hearts, cast our case and care on God, knowing that God means well for us, knowing that God intends for us truly and fully to live! May each of us experience the liberating release that confession grants and the healing freedom that God's forgiveness bestows.

It is hardest of all to forgive ourselves. That is why it is so important that we receive and take into our lives God's gracious pardon of us. If God forgives us, how can we not forgive ourselves? This, too: out of God's abundant forgiveness we receive, we also can begin to forgive others. Thanks be to God for this inexpressible gift!

Psalm 52

I marvel more and more as to how Jesus did it. How did he maintain his humility and centeredness in the face of bullies and braggarts who cared little for anyone or anything except the consolidation of power, the accumulation of wealth, and the intimidation of any who would oppose them? How did Jesus restrain himself from exploiting his equality with God (Philippians 2)?

Psalm 52 pictures a similar scenario. There are people, the psalmist says and our own experience confirms, who use other people for their own purposes and ends, who do not care who they hurt, who step on others in order to climb to higher places themselves, and for whom decency and dignity are absent concepts and practices.

But then there also are those who live as children of God, perhaps never acquiring many earthly riches nor much popular acclaim. But they trust in God's eternal love and, *"like a green olive tree,"* quietly, unassumingly, and daily bring forth the comforting shade of compassion and the life-giving fruits of neighborliness, justice, and generosity toward others, and thus keep hope alive in the world. In regard to a life lived with integrity, kindness, and contentment, hubris finally is no match for humility. May we, may I, belong to the company of the latter.

Psalm 53

This psalmist muses on the foolishness of discounting or denouncing the existence or primacy of God. Sometimes intellectual snobbery precludes a person from believing that God "is." ("I don't need an imaginary friend." "I can figure everything out myself." "Mortals are the measure of all things.") Sometimes it is a fierce desire not to be beholden to anyone, most of all to God, that causes people to dismiss, deny, or ignore God. Sometimes it is brazen sin that leaves people unwilling to be accountable to God for their unjust and untoward actions that offend against the neighborliness of God's kin-dom. Pride. Conceit. Narcissism. They say, in effect, *"There is no God."*

But too many others of us have experienced God and the grace of God in our lives to say there is no God. And when I consider other people I know and deeply respect who have trusted God profoundly both in life and in death, I cannot for a moment even begin to countenance the absence or non-existence of God.

But it is not only a question of whether I believe God is real. My unequivocal answer is yes. The more important question is whether I *live* as though I believe God is real.

Is the essence of my life, are my actions and priorities, congruent with what I say I believe about the loving presence of God in the world and in my life?

Let my "yes" be Yes!

Psalm 54

The superscription on Psalm 54 identifies it as a "prayer for vindication." Most of us have had the experience of being treated unfairly or having untrue accusations leveled against us or hearing others peddle a false narrative about us. They trump up false accusations against us or even outright betray us. We have had our actions both insidiously and insistently misinterpreted and misrepresented.

Mostly our attackers do these things to deflect attention from their own ethical, moral, or emotional misbehavior. They cover themselves in a cloak of victimhood and try to bend reality to fit the story they are seeking to sell.

It is tempting to answer our assailants in kind. But we best respond to others according to who we are and not who they are. We can commend those who would do us injury to God for care and "(re)constructive conversation."

"God is my helper; God is the upholder of my life," the psalmist testifies. As hard as it can be, we may with confidence trust that God will cause the "truth to out" and that we will be vindicated without resorting to "tit for tat" with those who would slay or slander us for their own benefit.

And, best of all, God knows the truth.

Psalm 55

I smile in recognition when I read and pray this psalm. Who hasn't shared at one time or another the sentiment of this psalmist?

"Oh that I had wings like a dove! I would fly away and be at rest; truly, I would flee far away; I would lodge in the wilderness..."

The psalmist had experienced treachery perpetrated by a close friend, family member, or colleague and it was deeply devastating. He wanted to flee, to escape, to run, to fly away from his pain and pathos. We sometimes find ourselves in situations from which we would like to make a similar exit.

But doing so seldom works, of course, except in cases of abuse, because the injury is not felt outside of us, but within us. We take it with us wherever we go, and wherever we go, there we are. There is no escape. We must face our suffering due to others' betrayal and feel it in all of its awful anguish. The psalmist encourages us to share our hurt with God and to trust that God will hold us and heal us:

"Cast your burden on the Lord, and the Lord will sustain you." Let God carry your burden. *"Come to me, all who are weary and carrying heavy burdens, and I will give you rest."*

God invites our deep honesty. Only then will we be able to receive God's compassion and care and begin to trust again that life ultimately is good and well worth living.

Psalm 56

The single sentence we are invited to believe in our deepest heart in all times, circumstances, and seasons of our lives is found in Psalm 56: *"This I know, that God is for me."*

Like unto it is a verse in St. Paul's Epistle to the Romans: *"If God is for us, who is against us?"*

The psalmist describes the persecution and strife he experiences at the hands of enemies, and sometimes even friends. But he roots himself in the even deeper experience of God's care, compassion, and love. He comes to know that God is for him. Such good news manages to calm him *("I am not afraid")* and to convince him that, both in life and in death, he belongs to God. That is the great truth from which the psalmist lives his life.

Whatever happens to us, nothing can separate us from the love of God. *Nothing can separate us from the love of God.* Even when we are chastened by God, it is for our own and/or our community's betterment. Even death is turned to life in the resurrection of Jesus Christ from the dead, a resurrection that, by God's grace, also includes us. *"This I know, that God is for me."* Remember it always, and live!

Psalm 57

In Romans 7, Paul confesses he does not understand his own actions: *"I do not do what I want, but I do the very thing I hate."* Our lusts and desires, the insatiable appetites of our egos, and our porous defense against temptations' allures all diminish our standing even in our own eyes.

Add to them external attacks - a friend's betrayal (as Saul turned against David), cruelty directed our way, unfair accusations lodged against us, plots hatched to undermine us, or social and economic realities that make life difficult

- and it is not hard to understand why we sometimes feel beaten down or lacking in hope.

This love song to God known as Psalm 57 urges us to set our hearts on God in whom we find our security and serenity. Then we will *"sing and make melody."* Neither safety nor fairness in this life can be guaranteed because life plays out with all of its turns and twists. But security *is* assured because, both at the beginning and at the end of our lives and every minute in between, we belong to God from whose eternal love there is never any separation.

Therein do we find the divinely-given peace that surpasses all understanding and lodges surely and securely in our heart when we are open to it, open to God. And thus we trust God's promise that God absolutely will accomplish God's purpose in us, through us.

Psalm 58

On first reading, there doesn't seem to be much to commend this psalm. There is not a lot that appears to be religious, spiritual, or even civil, about it. But only on first reading.

Looking again, we read of the psalmist's complete and utter frustration with *"you gods"* (vs. 1). That is a phrase referring to arrogant, unjust, and self-important earthly leaders who line their own pockets at the peoples' expense and who otherwise do violence in a hundred different ways to the *"bruised reeds and dimly burning wicks"* of society. We all should be as angry as this psalmist about such depravity.

Psalm 58 demonstrates that our prayers do not have to be polite or pious. Our prayers do not have to be prettified. We are invited to be honest in our praying, to cry from our depths about injustice and abuse inflicted on persons and peoples. We need, for instance, to be outraged about the racial antagonism directed against people of color and the growing economic disparity between rich and poor. We need to be scandalized by the atrocities hatred provokes.

I give this psalmist an A+ for descriptive and colorful language about what he wants God to do to the purveyors of vexation: *"Let them be like a snail that dissolves into slime."* That's good!

By psalm's end, though, this psalmist trusts God to resolve the incongruities and injustices of life in God's own way, often working through "righteous people" who are in league with God. Let us abide always with the God of steadfast and eternal love.

Psalm 59

One of the hallmarks of the Psalms is that there seems to be enemies all around. Some of them are external and pose a physical menace. Others threaten financial ruin. Still others are internal and weaken our self-esteem, confidence, or mental and emotional well-being.

The psalmists' enemies have been nations and governments using people as pawns. They have been close friends who betray their friendship. They have been inner devils that eat away at the psalmists' sense of self-worth and confidence. Occasionally the enemies are physical constraints or limitations that lead to exasperation and deep frustration. Sometimes, it is the psalmist's own pride or arrogance. It goes without saying that we have similar enemies as the psalmist and, also, like the psalmist, we ourselves may act in such a way as to be someone else's enemy.

In Psalm 59, the psalmist several times works up a good head of steam about his current enemies that afflict, intimidate, and brutalize. But, then, the psalmist remembers: *"You laugh at them, O Lord."* No enemy, inner or external, is greater than God. So then the psalmist remembers, *"You have been a fortress for me and a refuge in my distress...the God who shows me steadfast love."*

The prophet Isaiah said, *"In returning (to God) and rest you shall be saved; in quietness and trust shall be your strength."* That is the heart of this psalmist's message, too. You are not alone, not now, not ever, never.

Psalm 60

We usually think of anger in a pejorative light. Not many of us like to be on the receiving end of someone's fury. Neither do we feel good about being ill-tempered ourselves.

But, on further reflection, anger is not always bad, negative, or harmful. I recall my parents on more than a few occasions as I was growing up being angry with me. But they never brutalized me with their anger. And they did not misappropriate their anger, taking out on me their own frustration over situations having nothing to do with me at all.

Their anger had my best interest at heart. If administered fairly and nonviolently, anger directed at us can be a sign of love and care. I received my parents' occasional anger that way because their love for me was unmistakable. I didn't rejoice in their anger in the moment, but in the big picture and over the long haul it helped to form and shape my life, making me a better person than if they had adopted an "anything goes" posture and did not really care how my life turned out.

This psalmist sees the restorative potential of divine wrath. He trusts that God's anger never is ultimate, destructive, or final. He sees it as a tool God sometimes uses to steer us toward our best life in which we love God and serve and love our neighbors as ourselves. God always is angered by injustice and those who traffic in it. God's wrath, though, is not meant as punishment but as correction, compassion, and conversion.

How blessed we are to have such a sublimely wise and inexpressibly great God!

Psalm 61

In this psalm attributed to David, he imaginatively asks that God lead him to stand on a rock that is higher than he can attain by himself. He acknowledges that God is his refuge, the tall tower from which God can provide both protection and wisdom for David's life. Salvation is not his own doing, but God's.

But I am a little suspicious of a phrase that gets bandied about in Christian circles far too often and far too glibly for my taste. I raise my eyebrows a bit whenever I hear people urging "a personal relationship with God" or talking about "a personal relationship with Christ."

It's certainly not that such a relationship isn't possible or commendable or even necessary as we engage in various disciplines of prayer and service. But each of us is a part of God's larger concern - the Beloved Community, the kingdom/kin-dom of God, the body of Christ. *"Love God,"* says the new commandment Jesus gave, *"and love your neighbors as yourself."* Not "as much as yourself" but *as* yourself! God's concern for each of us is inextricably linked with God's concern for all of us.

Thus, as Psalm 61 demonstrates when David prays for the life and well-being of the king and thus, also, for the king's people, prayer that begins with personal cares grows into prayer for communal and community concerns. We cannot pray for life to be well for us without praying the same for others. We cannot pray for justice for ourselves without praying for justice for all. Likewise, prayers for the larger community naturally spill over and include us. We cannot have a personal relationship with God without it being concurrently communal and social.

We cannot be satisfied only to have a personal relationship with God since God wills us all to be a part of the Beloved Community together. Thus our prayer properly is expansive and inclusive and leads us to live as large as we pray.

Psalm 62

Psalm 62 is a heavyweight psalm. It is replete with sacred wisdom, devotion, and deep truth about the nature and character of God. *"God is my mighty rock, my refuge, my fortress, my hope, my salvation."* Since God is sovereign, the psalmist exhorts us to trust in God at all times no matter our situation or circumstance, communities as well as individuals. Yes!

But what leapt out at me as I read the psalm is found in the very first sentence: *"For God alone my soul waits in silence..."*

Silence. Silence is a scary word for many of us. We like to fill our waking hours with activity and distraction of all sorts. But because God often "speaks" in a *"still, small voice,"* cultivated times of silence are essential if we are going to "hear" God. I have a pastor friend, now deceased, who, with his wife, took a long prayer-walk, often in woods or forest but sometimes in the mountains or on a beach, every Monday. They agreed not to talk at all with each other while doing so. They broke their silence only after concluding their sojourn, usually over a picnic lunch they had carried with them, and it was only then that they shared what they had "heard" in the silence.

We often think prayer is what we say to God. But the real power of prayer most often is experienced in what God "says" to us. The divine voice usually is not audible to our ears. God more often speaks through something like inspired awareness to our souls or, sometimes, through another person's voice. Daily silence and stillness are required so that we may receive what God desires so much to give to us.

Not for our many words are we met by God in prayer but by the attention and open heart we offer to God. It is that open heart and attention to God, often in silence, that will help to keep us from giving into the many trendy allures, quick fixes, and cultural fads that, like a 4th of July sparkler, burn hot for a brief time and then burn out. *"God is my mighty rock, my refuge, my fortress, my hope, my salvation."*

Psalm 63

Blessed are those who know their lives have first and last to do with God. There can be little dispute that the human soul, every human soul whether we acknowledge it or not, thirsts for God.

Some of us, like the psalmist, behold God in the sanctuary as we give our hearts in communal worship. Perhaps God speaks to us through the gathered community itself. Maybe it happens via a line in a hymn, or a sentence in a sermon, or in the act of breaking bread and drinking wine together.

God also can be witnessed in God's magnificent creation, in every truly loving relationship, and in every act of justice that liberates people from oppressive systems and situations.

But, wherever and however it is that we offer our hearts and souls to God, and wherever it is that God finds us, our communion with God is the one thing necessary for us to live at peace...with ourselves, with others, and with the God of our lives.

God alone can satisfy our souls.

"O God, you are my God; I seek you; my soul thirsts for you; my flesh faints for you, as in a dry and weary land where there is no water."

Psalm 64

The old maxim that many parents tell their children at some point along the way - "sticks and stones can break my bones but words can never hurt me" - isn't even remotely true. We know it. Our broken bones, should we be unlucky enough to suffer such, typically heal in about six to eight weeks. But the sting and effects of words that speak ill of us can last a lifetime if we let them.

Our psalmist complains about those *"who aim bitter words like arrows."* When someone speaks unfairly of us or malevolently without reason, when others project their own insecurities onto us in fabrications or jealousies, when persons focus on the speck in our eye while they lumber about with a log in theirs, the emotional, spiritual, or psychological damage inflicted on us can be considerable. (The same is true, of course, if we do it to others.)

The psalmist's suggested remedy? Do not respond in kind, for, metaphorically, *"God will shoot his arrow at them and they will be wounded."* In other words, God will deal with them in God's own way.

So, take refuge and confidence in the One whose name for us is definitive and final: "Beloved."

Psalm 65

This psalm is a festival of praise to the God of our lives!

Do you make time in your life when, like this psalmist, you do nothing but serenade God with your exclamations and prayers of grateful praise? Certainly God is ready to hear about the pain and hurt in our lives, about the incongruities of life and what seems like blatant unfairness, our confessions of sin, our pleas for help, our intercessions for others, and our cries for justice whenever and wherever it goes missing.

The gospel assures us that in all of these circumstances and petitions, God reaches out to gather us under her wings as a mother hen sheltering her brood.

But, sometimes, it does us well to offer to God a full-throated paean of praise, not because God requires us to do it but because *we* need to do it. Spend time reflecting on the praiseworthy things God has done and is doing in your life and also in the wider world (*"O God of our salvation; you are the hope of all the ends of the earth…"*). Thankfully, praising God does not reduce our field of concern but expands it and deepens it, for God is the God of all. Let loose, for not only is it right to give God who gives us so much our thanks and praise, but it lifts us into a good and soulful place and deepens our relationship with God's world all around us.

Psalm 66

When I was a boy living in York, Pennsylvania, my parents in the summer months arranged for us to host a "Fresh Air Kid." The Fresh Air Fund was a program in which children in disadvantaged situations from New York City would be matched for two weeks with willing families who lived in less metropolitan places. One year, we hosted a boy named Arthur who was ten years old, my age at the time.

We stayed around our home doing day trips and "normal things" the first week Arthur was with us. The second week we went on a family vacation to Cape Cod. But no matter where we were or what we did, Arthur's refrain always was the same: "I can't believe how spacious it is here. I feel so alive here!" He must have said it four hundred times during his stay with us.

Our psalmist lists some tough spots and perilous circumstances his people had experienced throughout their history and then affirms, *"Yet you, O God, have brought us out to a spacious place."*

For Arthur, spaciousness was a kind of salvation. That seems to me a good way to describe the salvation of God as well: "salvation as spaciousness." God gives us "room" to turn our lives around, to turn toward God, to be freed from *"the weight and sin that clings so closely,"* and to take up robust residence in the spacious grace of the Beloved Community.

The spacious truth is that we are not closed in with God but opened up to the truth, wonder, and beauty that God has created and prepared for us.

Psalm 67

Notice the language in this psalm is in every instance about "us," not "me." It is about nations, not individuals.

It is not that individuals are unimportant to God. No, not that. It is, rather, that to a large extent, as a nation goes, so go the people and the individuals who live in it.

The psalmist prays to God that *"your way may be known upon earth."* The Hebrew prophets remind us that as a nation is guided by God's priorities and perspectives, it ultimately will be well for that nation and for those who live there. It will be a nation in which *"justice flows down like mighty waters and righteousness like an ever-flowing stream."* But a nation comprised mainly of individuals and leaders seeking only personal advantage, benefit, and privilege will be severely compromised and will falter, fail, and finally fall apart from the inside out.

Prayer for one's nation ought not to be for supremacy and superiority but servanthood and succor. For when God's ways are sacrificed on the bonfires of vanity, everyone suffers as the nation groans and trembles in tumult. But when even the most vulnerable among us are cared for and attended, as God desires, the nation thrives.

"May God be gracious to us and bless us and make God's face to shine upon us." Amen!

Psalm 68

There is a line in Maltbie Babcock's well-known hymn, "This Is My Father's World," that is a helpful interpretive lens through which to appreciate this psalm: *"Though the wrong seems oft' so strong, God is the ruler yet."*

There are people who believe that those who live obliviously and in opposition to God and God's ways have God on the ropes these days, that God is beleaguered and on the defensive, that God can be disregarded with impunity, that God is irrelevant, or that God is in a struggle with enemies, the outcome of which is yet to be determined.

But that is not true. There still is injustice in the world along with greed, bigotry, and inhospitality because there yet are those who have not found the joy in yielding to the wisdom, will, and ways of God. But to think that the ultimate fulfillment of God's kin-dom, therefore, is in jeopardy, is in error.

Psalm 68 is a close kin to Psalm 2 in which the psalmist says of those who believe they can outdo or outlast God, *"God in the heavens laughs; the Lord has them in derision."* *"Though the wrong seems oft' so strong, God is the ruler yet."* Indeed!

The resurrection of Jesus Christ confirms this psalm's affirmation of the triumph of God. The resurrection is the vindication of God's ways in the world for all time. Our lives are misspent when we try to live in any other way. The psalmist's strong advice is essentially the same as my grandfather gave to me when I was being obtuse or oppositional: "Get with the program!"

Then, our daily exclamations will mirror this psalmist's: *"Blessed be God!"*

Psalm 69

The psalmist is in a desperate way: *"I sink in deep mire, where there is no foothold; I have come into deep waters, and the flood sweeps over me. I am weary with my crying; my throat is parched. My eyes grow dim with waiting for my God."*

The psalmist has tried to remain faithful to God and God's ways in the world, albeit imperfectly, as perfection escapes every human being. But, fidelity to God's ways often is costly because they are at odds with many of the world's ways. God's ways, and those who seek to be faithful to them, are not received well by those in love and league with the world's values. Thus, the psalmist suffers reproaches, rebukes, and rough treatment by those who think the psalmist and his righteous ways are delusional at best or threatening at worst. The psalmist is undone.

While praying for relief for himself, the psalmist also prays that the ill-treatment he suffers because of his steadfastness to God not be an obstacle to those who would be drawn to the life of faith and who would place their hope in God.

For Christians, we best see the heart and ways of God in the life, ministry, teachings, death, and resurrection of Jesus. He upended conventional religious wisdom. He brought low the narcissists and hypocrites who used religious jargon and ritual for self-serving cover for their own plans. He exposed purveyors of injustice who feather their own nests with money, privilege, and power acquired at the expense of poor and powerless persons. Alas, he suffered for it, too, immensely, ending in crucifixion. But, finally, Jesus was vindicated by God in the resurrection.

For churches and individuals who dare to engage the radical love and hospitality of the Lord in the service of the gospel of Jesus Christ, we may expect to bear similar insults and scrutiny as both this psalmist and Jesus did. But, like Jesus, we cannot permit such "noise" to stop us or even to slow us down.

God's kingdom/kin-dom/Beloved Community will not be built by cowards and compromisers but by those who persist in embracing and responding to the Spirited call of God.

Psalm 70

Psalm 70 is a very brief prayer, but it contains this significant cry: *"O Lord, make haste to help me."* Make haste.

For those who are oppressed, distressed, dispossessed, or experiencing other systemic persecution, there is an urgency for relief and healing that those of means and privilege often do not sense or feel. It is not enough to say to those calling and praying for help, "It will get better someday. Be patient."

The Reverend Dr. Martin Luther King, Jr. wrote his prophetic "Letter from Birmingham Jail" largely to white moderates who nominally were on the side of his righteous cause but who had told him not to push too fast, too hard, or too far. King told them they could not from their privileged positions in society set the timetable for aggrieved people's freedom from injustice and domination.

It is not enough to say to those who are suffering the hurt and harm of bigotry, poverty, inequality, or any other desperate condition or circumstance, that life eventually will get better and that heaven will be their hoped-for haven. Those who do so are trying to escape their own culpability and desire not to see the present favorable arrangements of society that benefit themselves change. No! The gospel is first of all for *this* life, *this* world, *this* present time, heralding a quality of life betokened by the Beloved Community that starts here, now! We belong to a God who acts within history on behalf of those who are vulnerable and downtrodden, those who know themselves to be in need of help or assistance, many times through no fault or cause of their own.

That is the God we are called to follow!

Psalm 71

Twice in Psalm 71 the psalmist petitions God not to forget him in his later years:

"Do not cast me off, O God, in the time of old age; do not forsake me when my strength is spent."

"So even to old age and gray hairs, O God, do not forsake me..."

So many times during the course of my years as a pastor I have heard people as they grow older express similar sentiments and kindred prayers. They are concerned about being constrained by diminishing faculties and waning energy. They are anxious about a faltering ability to keep up with the world in the way they did in younger years. They are fearful of a mental decline or of a worrisome physical diagnosis. They are afraid of people taking advantage of them. They are frightened, as one older person recently said to me, "of feeling irrelevant or being useless or left behind." One's mortality is more on the mind than in younger years. My own mother, in the ninety-first and last year of her life said, "I'm not the girl I used to be." I imagined God responding to her, "But you're still my Jean whom I love."

In the more reflective evening of our lives, we can remember and recall all of the ways God has been for us, has helped us, and strengthened us in times of weakness or darkness. The psalmist re-commits to telling of, and witnessing to, the grace and mercy of our God.

This psalm assures that usefulness is no criterion to being loved by God. We are not loved by God, not at any age, because of what we can do but simply for who we are...a child of God. Even when our lives and years are far spent, God looks at us and says, "Mine!"

Psalm 72

This prophetic psalm asks God to give our leaders especially, but all of us generally, the capacity, artistry, and will to express and to show forth the grace, compassion, and justice of God in our lives that we see most definitively in Jesus Christ. It is the psalm par excellence to pray when we want to pray for our country and, indeed, for the whole world.

Our leaders - presidents and members of the Congress, governors, mayors, teachers, judges, clergy, business executives, celebrities, sports heroes, and parents, among others - have a responsibility to do on earth as it is said to be done in the kin-dom/kingdom of heaven. Justice and advocacy for all in need of them, help and assistance for all who require them, and a genuine equality of dignity and opportunity for all peoples and each person must be modeled by our leaders and become the practice of us all.

In the Beloved Community, life is to be gentle, the psalmist says, *"like rain that falls on the mown grass"* and tender like *"showers that water the earth." "Righteousness is to flourish and peace abound until the moon is no more."*

While the final verse of this psalm suggests that David wrote this prayer for his son, Solomon, the psalm, from a Christian perspective also prefigures Christ the King.

"Amen and Amen" are this psalmist's final words. "Yes and Yes," he declares, to all of God's ways, even as God has said "yes!" to us in Jesus Christ. *"Thy will be done on earth as it is in heaven."*

Live in God's ways so that *"God's glory may fill the whole earth"* and it may be well for all.

I love the Psalms because they're real...they're poetic...they summarize the Bible...they're prayers.

~ Hanna Hansen

Participation in communal life symbolized by worship and adherence to the teachings that guide personal behavior are of a piece. Both participation in public worship and personal discipline matter: honoring God in public must be accompanied by following God's moral precepts...God will see through insincere public shows of faithlessness if individuals privately act as thieves, adulterers, or slanderers of their kin and neighbors.

~ Ellen T. Charry

Psalm 73

Of all the psalms, Psalm 73 is near the top of my list of favorites. At least it cradles one of the verses I most cherish.

The first sixteen verses of the psalm describe a world we see every day - unethical people prospering, arrogant people living "the good life," immoral or unfeeling people stepping on others to climb higher themselves, people with no end or bounds to their lying and cheating, and all of it apparently going unpunished and sometimes even seemingly rewarded - while the righteous ones, the compassionate ones, those who are vulnerable or financially disadvantaged, and those seeking to live the gospel in their lives, suffer. Maybe it doesn't always happen this way, but too often it seems like it.

The psalmist was beside himself. He spoke for many of us when he fumed: *"When I thought about how I could understand a world arranged like this, it seemed to me a wearisome task...until...* (here's the verse...drum roll, please) *...I entered into the sanctuary of God, the intimacy of God. Then I understood."*

Yes! It certainly is true of my experience (though I concede others have had hurtful experiences in churches that speak religious language cloaked in the world's ways). It is in our life together, in true and authentic worship and the cumulative proclamation of the gospel, the hymns and songs and anthems of faith, the communion of persons seeking to enflesh and embody God's Beloved Community, that life begins to make sense and to take holy shape. It is in the gathering of God's people for worship, whether it be inside a building, a forest amphitheater, a home, or some other place, that we are given a glimpse, and an assurance, of the full and final triumph of God!

The psalmist concludes: *"It is good to be near God!"* Yes! Yes it is!

Psalm 74

Psalm 74 is a prayer offered in a time of national catastrophe and humiliation. The Babylonians had sacked Jerusalem, plundered the temple, and carried off many of the Israelites into exile. As the temple in Jerusalem was the center of life for Israel and the place where they believed God to dwell on earth, its destruction was a calamity of epic proportions. This psalm prayer asks God to remember Israel, to honor the covenant of salvation God has made with the ancient Israelites, to turn back Israel's foes, to heal the country, and to bring order out of chaos.

Our American nation today suffers no less a catastrophe and humiliation. What else can we call it when so-called "minority persons" are targets of the violence of hate? When equal justice under the law is compromised daily for people of color? When poverty rages in a land of plenty? When profiteering from the earth's resources is seen to be of greater importance than protecting it? When quality and accessible health care seems more a privilege than a right? When false teachers and secular anthems preach their seductive philosophies that see us chase after lesser gods and lower goals?

Like the psalmist, we, too, pray for God's forbearance and help. Like the psalmist, we, too, remember how God has acted for the benefit of God's faithful people in the past and trust that God will do so yet again. Like the psalmist, we trust that in a suffering society God is manifesting something new, a Beloved Community.

And we are invited to join God in bringing it into full bloom.

Psalm 75

Many people wonder why they should live in accord with God's ways and stand against persecution and injustice if God is going to execute justice and bring the peaceable kingdom to full flower anyway, as God declares in this psalm: *"When the earth totters, with all its inhabitants, it is I who keep its pillars steady."*

Why? Gratitude. Compassion, too. Love of neighbor. What God is going to do is what God always has done. From the time God delivered the ancient Israelites from their bondage in Egypt, God has acted to liberate and free God's people from every kind of stultifying and damaging captivity. And, supremely in Christ, we are granted release from our sins and from many other weights and burdens that cling so closely so that we may live justly, kindly, and humbly, so that we may live into the ministry of reconciliation we are given. True thanks-giving for God's grace and mercy translates into thanks-living.

Even more, God uses our grateful, compassionate, and re-directed lives to be a part of God's encompassing triumph. The life-giving gifts we receive from God are a trust and are to be used by us for the sake and benefit of all God's people.

For what higher or better end can we spend our lives than contributing to the kin-dom of God that is God's plan and intention coming to fruition?

Psalm 76

It cannot be made any clearer than Psalm 76: God cares for all but is especially concerned for those who are financially poor, systemically and systematically oppressed, emotionally compromised, or socially vulnerable. God also cares deeply for those who are lonely, confused, or ill of mind or body.

Historically, parts of the Christian church have highlighted personal and individual sin and thus have talked almost exclusively about a "personal Savior." More frequently neglected is the public and structural sin that makes life exceedingly difficult for those mentioned above. Power and wealth often are at the root of systemic injustice because of the way they are acquired, because they go unshared with those who have little or no access to them, and because those who are advantaged by them do not want their privilege to be endangered in any way.

Psalm 76 affirms that God will permit neither government, military power, nor individuals engaged in the abrogation of human rights, finally to stand. Where human wrath wreaks havoc, even going so far as to put Christ on the cross, God works justice, vindication, and glory for those trodden down.

With whom will you side? In whom do you put your trust? In whom do you have faith? On whom and for whom will you spend your life?

Psalm 77

Happily, there is not just one single way in which we may approach God in prayer. We do not have to scrub our moods or sanitize our speech. We do not have to be eloquent. We do not have to feign religiosity or piety or pose as someone we aren't. We do not have to be formal or fancy.

This psalmist is in distress as he begins his prayer. He doesn't wait until he gets himself together or until he can gussy-up his situation. He tells God his soul is discomfited. His heart is hurting or, maybe even worse, he feels nothing at all. He asks if God has forgotten how to be gracious and if God's promises are no longer in effect.

As his prayer continues, however, the psalmist remembers God's track record, God's faithfulness through all the years, and how in times past the psalmist wept well into the night but God brought relief, renewal, and even joy with the break of day. He recalls how situations and circumstances that seemed impossible somehow got worked out with God's help. He rejoices in how often when there seemed to be no way to a solution, God made a way.

Begin in prayer wherever we are, this psalm assures, and God will meet us there. In fact, even before we pray, God is present with us and inclined toward us in grace and favor.

Psalm 78

This psalm is disturbing even as it is, alas, very true to life. It tells of God's wondrous deeds to help ancient Israel only to be followed by Israel's ingratitude and intransigence. Then came God's judgment, mercy, and forgiveness of the people, more deeds done by God on Israel's behalf, followed again by more ingratitude and intransigence. Repeat again, again, and yet again.

With our country's mass killings, bigoted attempts to suppress voting rights, grotesque income inequality, rampant poverty, curtailment of civil rights and women's rights, ecological devastation, demonization of the "other" and so many other miscarriages of justice, not to mention our own personal upheavals, it seems our own generation is right at home in this psalm.

Can we not learn from history? God is for us. God wants the world and all who live herein to flourish and thrive. Every action God takes, every one, is in the service of establishing harmony, peace, hope, and well-being among all people and peoples, and even the earth itself. We are part of a larger and ongoing story of which God is author and finisher or, as the Book of Hebrews says it, *"the pioneer and perfecter."* We are forever a part of that ongoing story and are included in God's good end. As the psalmist reminds us, we are to share that story, the story of God's love and mercy, with others so that they, like us, have an opportunity to become their full and best selves in the service of the Beloved Community.

Our appropriate response is to give God thanks and praise, not only with our lips, but with our manner of living that reflects, honors, and perpetuates the life and example of Jesus Christ in the world!

Psalm 79

The occasion for this outburst of a psalm is the almost total desecration and destruction of the Temple in Jerusalem by the Babylonians.

The psalmist is beyond angry and wants God to exact vengeance. The psalmist believes Israel's interests and God's priorities align, that God is on Israel's side. After all, it was the sacred Temple that Babylon pillaged. *"Do something, God! Get them. Pay them back for what they did."*

Yet, in verse 9, the psalmist also prays for God to forgive Israel's sin. Perhaps we are all so divided. We cry to high heaven when we are undone as at the heinous and horrific attack on our country on what we now remember as "9/11." But then we also call to mind the abomination of our national sin of bigotry and violence against indigenous peoples and people of color from the very beginning of our nation's history. We come back once again to that repeated theme in our nation's life, and our own, about crying over the unrighteous speck in another's eye while glossing over the giant log in our own.

Perhaps this psalm best serves as a reminder that humility becomes us. While it is good and right to pray candidly to God, God is not beholden to our rants just as God is not tethered to others' bellicosity toward us. Trusting God to find the right balance between judgment and mercy - for others and for us - and learning from God's decisions is a requisite part of growing in faith and spiritual maturity.

Psalm 80

Three times in this brief prayer the psalmist prays this pleading refrain: *"Restore us, O God; let your face shine, that we may be saved."*

Several of the psalms detail the utter devastation of Jerusalem at the hands of enemies and, with it, the destruction of the Temple. It was the Temple that had been the center of Jewish life, the place where Jewish lives found their orientation and meaning.

The Israelites trusted that nothing was beyond the ability of God to restore if God chose to do it. Restoration and rejuvenation are possible, sometimes in the most surprising ways, when in God's wisdom it seems best to do so. This psalm is an earnest prayer for the restoration of Israel, the "vine" that God had planted, nourished, and brought to fruitfulness before Israel's waywardness led to its fruit turning bitter.

God can restore and renew what has been lost or broken in us. God can restore nations and even Christ's church when they no longer seem to be working or relevant to current needs. We are invited and encouraged to make our prayers for restoration and renovation to God. Then be alert for the astonishing ways God accomplishes it when doing so fills God's purpose and delight. Sometimes restoration involves new forms, strategies, or behaviors, but it is glorious and life-giving restoration nonetheless!

Indeed, O God, let your face shine upon us! "Restore to us the joy of your salvation" (Psalm 51:12).

Psalm 81

Amid all of the clamor and confusion of these days, with such a huge cacophony of voices vying for our attention and allegiance, it is no wonder God's word gets crowded out in us.

It's why the psalmists so often speak of silence as imperative to prayer. We tend to think of prayer as what we say to God. It is that, of course, but only secondarily. Prayer is first of all God speaking to us *and* in us. It is not usually an audible voice but a "knowing" that wells up on the inside, an inner "voice" attributable to God's Spirit. Our failure to "listen" invites bewilderment and disorientation to take up residence in our lives and compromises our ability to live in the way God intends.

Psalm 81 reports God ruminating wistfully, *"O that my people would listen to me, that they (we) would walk in my ways!"*

As the rest of the psalm testifies, God has proved more than reliable and trustworthy through the ages. God brought the ancient Israelites out of their bondage in Egypt. In Jesus Christ, God suffered the cross for our sakes. God brought forth the church that we may *listen, love, learn, and serve together* in Christ's name. Yet, we have not always listened to God and have tried to substitute our own wisdom and ways. It doesn't work.

God is not against us, but for us. How deeply God hopes that we shall listen to God's "voice" and both accept and follow what God says to us. For, by it, God means to draw us deeply into the common good and our own good, God's good for all!

Psalm 82

What if instead of seeking to arrogate as much to ourselves as possible - wealth, privilege, prerogative - we are as zealous in making sure our neighbors near and far in need also have access to a just and flourishing life?

And what if we demand of our governments nothing less? Not gerrymandering or voter suppression to assure election victories or catering to special interests and lobbies to fill campaign coffers or deporting persons without due process, but laws that care, support, and fairly protect everyone, everyone, everyone in common cause.

Psalm 82 makes the harrowing observation that *"all the foundations of the earth are shaken."* We know it, too. We live in times of high anxiety and suffering. Why? Because, the psalm says, and it still is so, the privileged and the powerful, the conniving and the connected, prefer dominance and self-interest to compassion and communal concern.

But, the psalm says, the world belongs to God who will not be mocked. As long as the weak are prey for prosperous predators, earthly kingdoms will continue to totter. The way to peace and well-being is through compassion and justice for all. That, the Lord says, is non-negotiable. *"Do justice, love mercy, walk humbly."* That is God's way and it is to be our way, too.

Psalm 83

Every nation, as long as it deals justly with other nations and its own people, has the right to feel safe from external attack. When this psalm first was prayed, Israel had been decimated by enemies. Israel's calls for God to avenge its foes certainly are understandable and viscerally felt. Many of us pray similar imprecations today about national foes, political adversaries, and personal enemies and demons. *"Let them be put to shame and dismayed forever; let them perish in disgrace."*

Israel's enemies mostly were external to it, foreign invaders. But it is no less difficult, and even more so, when a nation's enemies come from within, from within its own leadership, when its leaders care more for their own well-being and power than the nation they were elected or appointed to serve.

But God is God and does not have to do what Israel, or any other nation, or even we ourselves, demand. God listens to our outrage and hears our protests before handling injustice, danger, and heartache in God's own way.

In the end, after Israel's full-throated pique, the psalmist acknowledges that God is God of the whole earth and judges in divine ways that bring order and offer hope. It is up to us as nations, as peoples, as individuals, to follow and to trust our faithful God, whom Christians know best in Christ Jesus.

Psalm 84

Life for Christians isn't primarily about living in accord with Christian principles, concepts, ideas, or even theology. It's about living in relationship with and to Jesus Christ. As Jesus said, *"Abide in me as I abide in you. Just as the branch cannot bear fruit by itself unless it abides in the vine, neither can you unless you abide in me"* (John 15:4).

Thus, worship takes on central importance in the life of faith because it is where those related to Christ meet together to sing, pray, praise, learn, commune, and to give our hearts - both our own hearts and the heart of our community - to God and to one another.

The sanctuary isn't the only place we meet God, of course, but it is a primary place. It doesn't have to be located in a church building but is a space where the worshiping community gathers, where the Word of God can be heard and interpreted, where we are taught that friendship with Christ means extending amity and neighborliness to all God's children. It is where we are told of the Holy Spirit being poured out on us to prepare us to live in the world as followers and companions of Christ.

No wonder this psalmist cries out, *"I would rather be a doorkeeper in the house of my God than to live luxuriously in the tents of wickedness."* Oranges do not grow on apple trees and pears do not grow on olive trees. Just so, the fruits of God's Spirit are to be found and conveyed in a relationship with God that is curated in worship.

Rather than being blown back and forth on the changing winds of cultural trends and values, the overarching and eternal meaning for, and of, our lives is made and developed when we worship God in a community of God's beloveds.

Psalm 85

One of the loveliest images in the Psalms and in all of scripture, for that matter, is found in Psalm 85: *"Steadfast love and faithfulness will meet; righteousness and peace will kiss each other."*

These are attributes of God that are the means God uses in relating to us. Not surprisingly, they also are the attributes of the kingdom/kin-dom of God that God is calling forth among us and is inviting us to embody in the world. It takes courage to turn from the ways and values of the world in favor of living the hopeful and humble life God desires for us to live amid many competing claims and challenges. But it is essential if we are to become truly and fully human and if the world is to become "the peaceable kin-dom."

Some might argue that these attributes and ways to guide us in life aren't practical in today's world. I wholeheartedly disagree and, with the psalmist, I am fully convinced they are the only ones that really finally are.

Psalm 86

In a psalm full of prayer petitions to God, many of them asking for help against the *"insolent band of ruffians that rise up against me,"* it turns out the most serious enemy doesn't come from without but within: *"Give me an undivided heart, O God, to revere your name."*

A divided, duplicitous, or double heart is deeply injurious to a life of faith. A divided, duplicitous, or double heart strains our relationships, not only with God, but also with other people. The gospels tell us, for instance, that *"we cannot serve two masters...we cannot love both God and mammon"* (money/wealth).

When someone or something other than God becomes more, or even as important to us, as God, our divided heart weakens and dissipates all of our loves and commitments. In the Beatitudes, when Jesus said, *"Blessed are the pure in heart,"* the best word to define "pure" is "singleness." "Blessed are those with singleness of heart." When God is our primary love and devotion, such single-heartedness arranges all of our other loves in their proper places and perspectives and enables us to embrace and to do justice to them all. Singleness of heart is tantamount to wholeheartedness. It leads both to God's joy and ours. Amid a chorus of petitions in the psalm, pleas for help, they find their commonality in the need for an undivided heart.

"Teach me your way, O Lord, that I may walk in your truth; give me an undivided heart to revere your name. I will give thanks to you, O Lord my God, with my whole heart..."

Psalm 87

It is not unusual for a child, orphaned at a very young age, to come to a time when that child wants to know not only the identity of its biological parents but something about them.

That certainly is understandable. But Psalm 87 insists that our new birth into citizenship in the kin-dom of God is even more determinative and defining for our lives. Parents are very important, of course, but God's acts of creating us and loving us all our days are primary.

As grateful as I am and always will be for my parents and all they did for me, gave me, taught me, and for how much they loved me, it is my baptism into Christ and my life in the midst of worshiping communities that have been the most significant gifts of my life. The contents of my birth certificate - name, parents' names, earthly location and date of birth - bless me but reading in this psalm that God lists me in God's celebratory register is pure and unutterable joy. You are in that register, too, a full-fledged citizen of God's family!

No matter our life's circumstances, we always, by the grace of God, are both free and wise to live life fully as the beloved children of God we are! Nothing will give us greater joy!

Psalm 88

Psalm 88 is a mess of unrelieved misery and despondency. Everything that could go wrong for the psalmist does and God gets blamed for a lot of it. The psalmist's soul is troubled, his friends have abandoned him, his heart is cast down, his life seems purposeless, and he feels brushed aside even by God. Have you, as I have, ever been there?

The psalmist feels helpless. But still he prays which is in itself a sign that he yet believes his life has first, foremost, and forever to do with God. Jesus felt deep agony, too, and prayed from the cross, *"Why, O God, have you forsaken me?"* before also praying, *"Father, into your hands I commend my spirit."*

Even when we *see "as in a glass dimly,"* even when everything seems sorrowful or sad, even when we have a difficult time making any sense of life, praying to God in whatever way we can, even in a Psalm 88 manner, will keep hope alive in us until our weeping and mourning turn into laughing and dancing, which is a promise of God to us.

Psalm 89

Psalm 89 feels like an Easter psalm! In it, the psalmist depicts God promising that King David's line will continue forever and that God never will break the covenant made with God's people.

The line and lineage of David find their apex in Jesus Christ whom God raised from the dead as vindication and confirmation that the ways and teachings of Jesus are God's ways. Thus, they also are to be our ways, too.

Much of the psalm is an extended "Hallelujah!" to match our Easter "Alleluias." Though trial, trouble, temptation, or tumult occasionally find us, and sometimes even may be signs of God's judgment, they are not signs that God is forsaking us. We do not always understand why life happens as it does (*"now we see only in part..."*), but the difficult times are never because God's love is conditional. We may not always comprehend God and God's ways, but this is sure: God never wavers in God's love for us. Through all of the changing seasons and circumstances of life, God is with us.

The first two verses of this psalm provide the context for the rest of it and for our lives, the psalmist affirming of God, *"I will sing of your steadfast love, O Lord, forever; with my mouth I will proclaim your faithfulness to all generations. I declare that your steadfast love is established forever; your faithfulness is as firm as the heavens."*

In the difficult times of our lives, either of our own doing or from beyond us, we are invited to remember and to keep close to our hearts this confession of faith in the God who loves us now and forever, *whose love knows no end.*

Thy word is a lamp unto my feet and a light unto my path.

~ Psalm 119:105

Psalm 90

A friend said of my mother who lived into her nineties, "Think of all she has seen in her life," and then went on to recap many of the major events and inventions of the past century. But even the longest human life does not hold a candle to the eternal nature of God. God is not a modern invention. God is neither "trending" nor a fad, not like grass that withers or a flower that fades, Rather, God is the great reality in which all of life forever - backward and forward, without beginning and without end - is rooted and lived.

Thus, while we have this life upon the earth, precious in its relative brevity, we do well to allow that divine root that is God to nourish a good, just, and fruitful life in us in order *to gain a wise heart.* Wisdom is not philosophical or theoretical; wisdom is the practical day-to-day ability to live life well and in the way its Creator hopes and intends we live it. Thus are we given the stories and teachings of Jesus, the presence and power of the Holy Spirit, and even these psalms that we are in the midst of praying.

Part of gaining a wise heart is learning how foolish it is to live in any way contrary to God's good will. Like a child chastened by loving parents, *God's anger is contained within God's love.* God's wrath is not for our condemnation. When it comes to us, it is for our recalibration so that in our span of earthly years we may experience the joy of contributing to the flowering of God's kin-dom of peace, justice, and hope for all.

Psalm 91

A helpful lens through which to perceive and understand this psalm may be a stanza of John Newton's timeless hymn, "Amazing Grace":

"Through many dangers, toils, and snares, I have already come. 'Tis grace has brought me safe thus far, and grace will lead me home."

As were all of the psalms, this one originally was prayed in the midst of a worshiping congregation. As such, it is an affirmation of faith and trust in God, that God indeed is our refuge and our help. It is a psalm meant to affirm that the children of God ultimately are secure in God even if we are not always safe from harm in this earthly life. We are not promised a non-perilous pilgrimage through this life. We are promised that *nothing in all creation can separate us from the love of God in Christ Jesus*" (Romans 8:39).

No one was closer to God than Jesus and yet his life was taken unjustly. Nevertheless, he was secure in God who even in the midst of death gave life.

God is our eternal home and God's grace always will lead us there.

Psalm 92

"The righteous flourish like the palm tree, and grow like a cedar in Lebanon...In old age they still produce fruit; they are always green and full of sap..."

In our culture, youth is served. But, among the people of God, lives long lived in prayer, praise, worship, and service continue to offer God's blessings to the world that flow even through the valedictory years of these saints! It is beautiful to behold. Lifetimes of faith and faithfulness have not worn them out nor wearied them but are bearing evening fruit that helps the communities of which they are a part to thrive and renew, that enables the kin-dom of God to more fully manifest on earth.

As our years accumulate, questions about God asked in younger years are given a measure of insight and satisfaction via God's continuing faithfulness and steadfast love. As we grow in the wisdom of God shared with us by the Holy Spirit, we begin to "see" what had been hidden to our earlier perception. Since our lives best are understood in retrospect, a larger and more complete picture emerges in our evening years as we are able to survey the multiplicity of ways in which God has been present with us through thick and thin, ups and downs, mountaintops and valleys.

Our faith does not have an expiration date on it. Indeed, as the psalmist celebrates, *"in old age, we still produce fruit."*

Psalm 93

"Your decrees are very sure; holiness befits your house, O Lord, forevermore."

Holiness does not mean holier-than-thou. It is not false piety or platitude disguised as wisdom. It is not posting a politically oriented meme on social media. Holiness is not religion on parade. Holiness is God in us even as we live in God. *"Abide in me and I in you,"* says Jesus (John 15:4).

Because God is sovereign, God's decrees *"are very sure."* Thus, holiness is *"doing justice, loving kindness, and walking humbly with God."* Holiness is a daily practice, practicing the presence of God in all that we do and say. It is seeking to live with the mind of Christ and following in our lives the ways Jesus taught and demonstrated in his own life and death.

Holiness certainly is not dour or depressing. It is not restrictive or constrictive. It is just the opposite. Holiness is the full and expansive expression of life, freedom, and joy. Holiness *"befits God's house"* in which you and I and all the children of God are invited to make our home. Even when fear, hardship, sadness, or uncertainty seem to flood our lives, the holiness that is of God keeps us afloat until better days arrive.

God's decrees and blessings are very sure because God is very sure, eternal, and sovereign.

Psalm 94

The psalmist begins this prayer by calling on the *"God of vengeance"* to let loose on the proud, the arrogant, and the wicked, on those who blithely claim that the Lord neither *"sees nor perceives"* and who perpetrate their mayhem with abandon on innocent people.

God does not traffic in vengeance, though, but justice. God is a God of justice. God's ways will prevail finally, fully, and always. God simply and steadily does what God promises to do. The ways of the wicked will not stand. In God's time, injustices will be reversed. I love the way the late Old Testament theologian Walter Brueggemann put it: "Joy is the assurance that one day all of the incongruities of life will be resolved."

Thus we live by faith and not by sight. We cannot always see the end of a story but we can be confident that our stories find their fullness in the steadfast love of the Lord. The psalmist in his rage calls on God to wipe out the wicked but, fortunately, God is not obligated to obey our commands. Even those who work against God's ways - who trade away truth for privilege and faithfulness for personal advantage - while being held to account in the kingdom of God and liable to God's judgment and justice, yet are also within God's circle of redemption.

The praise of God finally expressed in this psalm is among the most beautiful in the Bible. The takeaway? We can rely on God and trust God completely as we live our days upon the earth. *"The Lord has become my stronghold and my God the rock of my refuge!"*

Psalm 95

Through seven joyous verses, the psalmist leads the people in the praise of God. But then he laments that they do not sufficiently hear and trust God's word in equal measure to their praise of it. He compares them to their ancestors who were delivered from their bondage in Egypt, provided safe passage through a parted sea, and promised a land flowing with milk, honey, and all manner of good and necessary things. Yet they groused and complained when water seemed in short supply, when the divinely-provided manna did not suit their taste, and whenever their journey required rigorous faith and robust fortitude.

Such willfulness leads to a soul as barren as the wilderness through which those ancient grumblers were traveling. But God is our Creator and cares for both the creation and for God's children in it without fail or exception. Thus, the psalmist exhorts the people to *"sing to the Lord...to make a joyful noise to the rock of our salvation...to come into God's presence with thanksgiving...to worship and bow down...to kneel before the Lord, our Maker...to listen to God's voice."*

If we do not carry with us into the world that which we acknowledge to be present in God's heart - mercy, justice, compassion, and unconditional love - both faith and life in us will falter. When it comes to God and God's ways, the old hymn has it right: "Trust and obey, for there's no other way." At least no other way that leads to fullness of life and deep joy.

Psalm 96

When my brothers and I were growing up, we would try to "work" our mother and father, promising to do something they wanted us to do just after we did what we wanted to do. "We'll clean our rooms as soon as we get home from playing baseball with our friends," we'd say. For a while, our strategy worked well for us until one day our mother, catching on to our lack of follow through, said, "I've heard that song before."

Thus ended our favorable arrangement. Thankfully, the new song our mother told us we'd be singing from that point on was not hurtful but helpful as we learned to be more reliable and responsible, not to mention more truthful.

"O sing to the Lord a new song," this psalm exclaims. No more of the same old attempts to prioritize and justify our actions and ways that are contrary to God's. We are invited to "sing a new tune" of joyous and willing fidelity to *"the One who is greatly to be praised"* and who *"judges the world with righteousness."*

A new song for a new hope and a renewed community of which to be a part! Let us "sing" it with trust and hope. Praise the Lord, indeed!

Psalm 97

"All servants of images are put to shame, those who make their boast in worthless idols..."

There long has been a quest to "find" the face of Jesus. Paintings, sculptures, and collaged images of Jesus have proliferated. An onslaught of different actors has portrayed Jesus on movie and television screens.

The search is understandable. We like to know what people look like as a part of getting to know them. But with that desire comes a caution. We often make assumptions about persons based on their appearances. We think we know them when we really do not.

That makes portrayals and images of God whom we cannot see problematic, as our psalmist obviously experienced in his congregation. There is a danger to making God in our image. Picturing God as an old, bearded man sitting on a celestial throne, for instance, is not at all helpful as it leads to false ideas about God. Picturing Jesus as a white man when he was not has led to persecutions of people of color.

Many of the reformers of the church in the fifteenth and sixteenth centuries did not approve of images of the

Divine because they believed they are too limiting; they compromise the "I-Thou" relationship between God and us as they put God on too-familiar footing. They are emblematic of our human desire to make the mysterious manageable (read: exercise control).

As the husband of an artist, I hasten to add that I do not believe the psalmist is calling for a halt to all artistic renderings of the Divine Mystery. But we are to take care not to worship or venerate them for the fullness of God cannot be conveyed or mediated by an image or images. Might a "God beyond images" help to forestall our attempts to make God in *our* own image? Might a "God beyond images" allow us to meet a God unrestrained by the fetters and boundaries of our human devising and understanding? Might a "God beyond images" open us more fully to the Holy Spirit and to follow where God, and not our cultural values, rightly leads us? Might we find in following a "God beyond images" true righteousness and cascading joy?

Psalm 98

Rising early enough in the morning to behold the dawn as it is beginning to break, and venturing outside for my morning walk, I am treated to a delightful symphony of birdsong as feathered companions of varied hue and voice sing their praise of a new day. Squirrels screeching as they skitter from tree branch to tree branch and chipmunks chattering as they race to and fro on the ground add their morning thanks and joy. In turn, my own praise of the One who created the morning and all of the creatures who awaken to it, is prompted and supported.

Psalm 98 makes abundantly clear that the preferred language of the reign of God and the Beloved Community is praise:

"Let the sea roar and all that fills it; the world and all who live in it. Let the floods clap their hands; let the hills sing together for joy...!"

It behooves us to become practiced and proficient in praise. It is my experience that offerings and outpourings of praise encourage the same in others. What a difference it makes in us, in our relationships, and in a wider community like a workplace, a church, a school, a family, or a city when praise and not insult, praise and not condemnation, praise and not self-aggrandizement, is on our lips and in our hearts. Imagine how it would transform the politics of this nation and its neighborliness.

When we praise God first of all, then praise all around is likely to follow and that, in turn, helps to make earth more like heaven. Joy to the world!

Psalm 99

I used to think "holy" and "holiness" were religious words that would make me stand out or stand apart in a way that would cause others to think more highly of me. Not that I ever actually had that problem, though, to be honest. I never approached what I would call "holiness" in that mistaken vein.

Today, I respect those words immensely. I aspire to holiness, to being holy. The problem, as this psalm makes clear, is that only God is holy. ("Holy, holy, holy, only Thou art holy" is a lyric from an old and wise hymn.) Holiness is a divine quality marked by steadfast love, radical hospitality, redemptive justice, and the grace of forgiveness.

Our brush with holiness comes in our relationship with God, a relationship affirmed in our baptism in which we are marked sacramentally as God's own forever. As we abide in God and God abides in us, holiness is conveyed to us. No matter how hard we try, we cannot make ourselves holy. Only God can make us holy, and does, as we then commit our lives to God in faith, hope, and love.

Psalm 100

In my humble opinion, if we are going to learn, know, commit to memory, and fall back on only one psalm, this psalm may well be the one! I understand a compelling case can be made for Psalm 23, Psalm 46, Psalm 51 and undoubtedly a few others, but, for me, it's "Old Hundredth." This psalm tells us just about all we need to know about God and our life of faith.

The worship and praise of God stand at the very center of our lives. The Lord of our lives isn't wealth, achievement, reputation, fame, family, or anything or anyone else but God. Why? *"It is God who made us and we belong to God; we are God's people, and the sheep of God's pasture."* Not only is God our Creator but God also is the One we are bidden to follow in our lives, a God Christians know best in Jesus Christ, but a God whose children all people are.

The proper stance toward God is gratitude. *"Enter God's gates with thanksgiving. Give thanks to God."* Not only does God give us the gift of our lives and a wise way to live, but *"the Lord is good; God's steadfast love endures forever, and God's faithfulness is to all generations."* God's faithfulness to us encourages our faithfulness to God and to all God's children.

Let us write this psalm on our hearts. Let it melt into the core of our whole being...and live!

Psalm 101

This psalm is one of the so-called "royal psalms" within the larger collection of psalms. Presumably it was sung by a king, quite possibly David, either at his coronation or at some other celebratory festival and is descriptive of the work and character of a good king. Eventually, Jesus embodied many of this psalm's exemplary attributes and they became prescriptive for all of us, for all God's people who live within the kingdom of God, the Beloved Community.

Clearly, the psalm says that ends do not justify means. How one does something is as important as what is accomplished. We accrue no credit by arriving at a good end by unscrupulous means.

"I will walk with integrity of heart."

"I will sing of loyalty and justice."

But, also:

"One who secretly slanders a neighbor...and has an arrogant heart, I will not tolerate."

What one believes is not insignificant but must be confirmed by the way one lives and what one does. "The proof of the pudding" as the saying goes, "is in the eating." Integrity, compassion, loyalty, kindness, mercy, and justice are the hallmarks and affirmations of a God-infused and God-pleasing life. How easy it is to sing a good song but then act in unsingable or unspeakable ways.

Lord, have mercy. Christ, have mercy. Lord, have mercy.

Psalm 102

Whether the psalmist in the first part of his psalm is desperately ill or suffering some other kind of anguish we are not told - *"I am like a little owl of the waste places...I am like a lonely bird on the housetop"* - but we know he is in a bad way. Perhaps it is that his sin has landed him in a bad place and separated him from love and meaningful interaction with others.

The second part of the psalm tells of his community's profound pain after the ransacking of Jerusalem and the trauma of exile. The psalmist gathers the peoples' distress and weariness into a plea for God to restore and to renew the community.

Finally, the psalmist acknowledges that even when everything seemingly is falling apart and life is out of kilter, God is the only reliable recourse. God made the world, knows intimately how it works, has demonstrated steadfast love and mercy in the past and, because God always is true to God, will do so again, and again.

This psalm is honest about the trials, tribulations, and troubles the people of God face, sometimes of their own doing and sometimes not. We are not immune from them. But the psalmist also is irrevocably convinced in faith and by his own experience that our ultimate hope and help is in God alone. I second the motion!

Psalm 103

The story of our faith did not start when we arrived on the scene. We are heirs to what is called a "received tradition." That is, our faith is part of a continuing story. It has a history. God has a track record. Our faith has a communal memory and testimony.

When this psalmist lets loose with his gushing fountain of praise, he is speaking not only from his own experience and observation but from that of the whole people of God over many centuries. Such a legacy helps to prevent the psalmist from giving up on faith. The psalmist is able to lead his congregation in trusting God even when circumstances become difficult, enigmatic, or heartrending.

It is good news that we do not have an untried, untested, unproven God! A long lineage of people in every time and place has witnessed God's incomparable grace, mercy, love, and compassion, a history in which we ourselves are blessed now to take our places! God's story did not begin with us. But, by God's grace, God's story includes us in its vast, eternal sweep! The psalmist attests that, though our lives in this world *are like grass, flourishing like a flower of the field before it is gone,* we are kept forever in God's everlasting love.

"Bless the Lord, O my soul, and all that is within me, bless God's holy name. Bless the Lord, O my soul, and do not forget all God's benefits..."

Psalm 104

This comprehensively powerful psalm celebrates a creation that is well-ordered and works together as a grand, unified whole. As created, it is a work of great beauty, purpose, and holiness.

I find it instructive that scripture refers not to nature, as we often do, but to Creator God and God's *creation*. The Hebrew language in which the psalms were written does not even have a word for "nature" in the way we typically use it.

It makes me wonder why we use the word "nature" so much in our conversations instead of "creation" or "God's creation." We say "we're going out into nature" instead of "we're going out into God's creation." Is it a collective attempt at some conscious or subconscious level to desacralize the creation so we can think and act as if we are in charge of it and do with it as we will instead of exercising judicious and reverent care and stewardship of it?

Perhaps if we talked less about nature and the natural world and more about God's creation with its supernal design, we would treat it more responsibly and respectfully. Perhaps we more readily and faithfully would befriend God's creation.

There really isn't anything natural about nature. It's all a divine creation. The noted reformer, John Calvin, called the creation "the theater of God's glory." And so it truly is! What a difference it makes in our lives when we think of it and treat it as such!

Psalm 105

"Seek God's presence continually."

This psalm recounts the "salvation history" of the Israelites as God delivered them from their bondage to Pharaoh and the Egyptians and led them into the life of freedom that God had promised them. There were many twists and turns along the way but God was in them all, always making a way when there seemed to be no way.

No matter the situation at hand or the conditions in which we find ourselves, God does no less for us. Practicing the presence of God - that is, trusting and seeking to discern the ways God is with us now - is both imperative and comforting as we seek to live faithfully as children of God and as a part of God's great kin-dom.

Never doubt God's presence nor God's willingness to help. It is not for no reason it is said that God works in mysterious ways. But those ways, obvious or obscure, are always and exactly the ones we need to set us on the path we are to go and to give us the help and guidance we need for living, loving, and serving in this world.

Psalm 106

One of the great, albeit largely unheralded, biblical words is *"nevertheless."*

"Nevertheless, while we were yet sinners, Christ died for us, was raised for us, and reigns in power for us."

"Nevertheless," the father's actions stated when the debauched prodigal returned home. Despite the son's actions and betrayals, the father said, *"Bring quickly the best robe and put it on him; put a ring on his finger and sandals on his feet. And get the fatted calf and kill it, and let us eat and celebrate; for this son of mine was dead and is alive again; he was lost and is found."*

There are many and various reasons why God would be justified in having nothing more to do with us. We regularly betray God and God's ways and offend against God's kin-dom. *Nevertheless,* God's love is solid and steadfast and will never, not ever, let us go.

Psalm 106 confirms that even amid the Israelites' track record of waywardness, sinfulness, and rebelliousness against God, *"Nevertheless, God regarded their distress when God heard their cry"* (v. 44).

All of us experience God's grace within God's great "nevertheless." Thanks be to God!

The Lord is my light and my salvation; whom shall I fear? The Lord is the stronghold of my life; of whom shall I be afraid?

~ Psalm 27:1 (NRSVUE)

Psalm 107

"*L*et those who are wise give heed to these things, and consider the steadfast love of the Lord."

Before he makes the summary statement I have quoted above, the psalmist catalogs a variety of ways people make life difficult for themselves and sometimes for those around them as well.

There are countless ways people find to complicate their lives, to careen toward catastrophe, or to crash against the rocks. Many of them have to do with forsaking the ways of God in a selfish or futile quest to satisfy their own appetites and ambitions. But, notice well that God ministers into whatever trouble the people manufacture for themselves. *"Then they cried to the Lord in their trouble, and God delivered them from their distress."*

In God's mercy, God chastens, but then hastens to provide us with yet another opportunity to live in harmony with God's design, teachings, and purpose. Wise are the ones who do so, the psalmist insists, who trust God's deep wisdom and indefatigable love, and who thus embark on the richest adventure life possibly can offer.

"Let those who are wise pay attention and consider the steadfast love of the Lord."

Psalm 108

This psalm at first blush seems to get it backward. Attributed to David, he said he will *"awake the dawn."* Usually it is the other way around. It's the dawn, the daylight, that awakens us.

But David isn't being literal here. He prays, *"My heart is steadfast, O God. I will sing and make melody. Awake my soul! I will awake the dawn."*

When our lives are grounded in God and we approach life with thanks and praise, life takes on a new and creative tone and tenor, much more fulfilling than when we gripe and grouse our way through our days and nights and act as if life owes us all manner of good things it has not yet delivered to us.

Praise and gratitude create "a new day" in our lives as they help us to focus on God and others instead of giving ourselves top billing and expecting to be served, rather than serving.

Waking the dawn, helping to usher in a "new day," a new way, God's way, strengthens God's kin-dom among us and leads to joy.

Psalm 109

Who might claim Psalm 109 as "their Psalm"?

Surely members of BIPOC (Black, Indigenous, People of Color) communities have reason to make this their psalm with their history of enslaved servitude, a criminal justice system historically and contemporarily arrayed against them, and proposed voter suppression laws that seek particularly to disenfranchise persons of color. Members of the LGBTQ+ community with too many state legislatures seeking to abrogate their civil and human rights have every reason to cry out in a similar vein as the psalmist. A woman who has been a victim of sexual aggression or assault likely would find empathetic expressions amid this psalm's cries for vengeance. People who have been falsely accused or unfairly persecuted can get as exasperated as this psalmist. People who live with chronic and debilitating medical maladies might understandably get worked up like our psalm-singer. As the rights of women to make decisions about their own bodies continue to be questioned and imperiled, they have cause to cry out in concert with this psalmist.

Most of us in our own lives likely have experienced personal circumstances that could make us a partner to this psalmist's heartrending cry.

To love our neighbors who cry out of the depths in their pain means to abide with them in their hurt, to join them in their desperate pleas and prayers to God, and to take actions congruent and congenial with God's heart and ways to help to alleviate their pain and to mitigate their painful circumstances. God is capable of acting alone but almost always chooses to work through God's faithful people.

In such a way does God's "new heaven and new earth" begin to transform the world, *and* us, too.

Psalm 110

This seemingly enigmatic psalm is the one the New Testament quotes more than any other. It originally was used in Old Testament times as a coronation prayer at the installation of a king. Eventually, the writers of the New Testament considered the resurrection of Jesus to be the fulfillment of this psalm...Christ our King.

What is the value and use of Psalm 110 to us today? It can be taken as a celebratory psalm for Jesus the King who, of course, put a much different spin on the practice of royal governance than the kings of nations typically exercised. Remember how Jesus answered Pilate's query about being a king by saying, *"My kingdom is not of this world"*?

As such, Jesus' kingship, or messiahship, has profound implications for his "subjects" or, better said, his community of followers, his "beloveds," his "friends" (John 15:15) in every age. The teachings, instructions, and commands of Jesus are not open to negotiation or amendment. They are binding but, also, happily, they are for the building up of

God's kingdom. Jesus the King came not to be served, but to serve. Thus, that is the model, too, for those for whom Christ is King and who find life in his gracious, merciful, and eternal reign.

Psalm 111

This psalm is not a celebration of the psalmist's good works, nor of ours. It is, rather, a love song praising God for all of God's wonderful acts and holiness, for God's wisdom and justice, and for God's saving grace by which sinners are forgiven and set free to live just and loving lives. *Great are the works of the Lord...*" We praise God not only when things are going well for us and thus we feel satisfied and happy. Even more, we praise God when we see and notice God's awesome works. Praise based on God's acts and not on the changing nature of our own feelings has the capacity to elevate our lives.

In my first church I served as a pastor after graduating from seminary, a leader in the congregation wanted to start what he called "The Grace Fund," a funding mechanism for mission. He asked me one day for my definition of "grace." Armed with my fresh theological degree, I said confidently, "God's unmerited favor bestowed on us." Jim responded, "That's what all you preachers say. No, that's too small." He then proceeded to educate me with his own definition. I have to admit it's the best definition of grace I've ever heard: "God's own life shared with us."

That is what this psalmist is so excited about. At God's initiative, we participate in God's life. Sometimes we are a bit too self-congratulatory about our "good works." For, the truth is, we are able to do "good works" because God is working in us and through us. This psalm gives an accounting of the good works of God. When God shares God's life with us and we are open to receiving God's grace, God's own life, those are the works in which we shall be engaged, too.

"Let the one who boasts, boast in the Lord" (2 Corinthians 10:17).

Psalm 112

Many times in their psalms the psalmists refer to the "wicked." But they used the word differently than we often mean it today.

When we call people "wicked" we typically mean they are evil monsters, depraved, beyond the bounds of civilized behavior. In the Psalms, "wicked" refers to those who conduct themselves in ways contrary to the ways and will of God. Wicked people may be very congenial even as they take advantage of and prey on those who are vulnerable instead of helping them.

The wicked use other people to try to make their own lives better and more secure. The wicked buttress their own standing by diminishing others. The wicked are those who do not have the interests of others in mind. The wicked are those who major in ulterior motives. The wicked are manipulators. They are schemers with their own enhancement in mind.

On the other hand, our psalmist says of those who trust God and follow God's ways:

"Happy are those who revere the Lord, who greatly delight in doing God's commandments...their hearts are steady."

May we have the courage, compassion, and conviction to be counted among these latter.

Psalm 113

"The Lord raises the poor from the dust and lifts the needy from the ash heap to make them sit with princes. Praise the Lord."

Some of God's greatest wonders include God making something good from a life that seemingly is going nowhere, or creating a path where there appears to be no possible way forward, or turning disappointment and grief into contentment and joy.

What if life never could change or heal? It would be a life without hope. But the good news of faith is that, with God, nothing is impossible!

There is no situation in our lives that is beyond God's reach, redemption, rehabilitation, or repair. The "fix" may not be immediate, but in its time it will be effective. We do not always know how God will do it, but *that* God will do it we can be certain.

If we trust the power of God to work newness in us, to help us to see God's ways and wisdom and to live accordingly, and to get us to give up our ham-fisted desire to control every aspect of our lives in favor of dancing with God's Spirit, we shall be astonished at how *"all things begin to work together for good."* Praise the Lord!

Psalm 114

The Exodus event in Israel's history is so formative and momentous - Israel's deliverance from the tyranny and terror of Pharaoh's Egyptian taskmasters - that it is presented in this psalm as having cosmic collaborators. Waters strategically recede to allow the Israelites to escape while mountains and hills skip like little children in celebration, and the fierce grip of empire collapses. The sovereignty of God is firmly evinced and evidenced.

Thus, the whole world is put on notice: *"Tremble, O earth, at the presence of the Lord..."* Not even the strongest nation is beyond God's reach or reproof when it strays from doing justice and loving mercy. The same holds true for individuals.

God yearns for all people to be fully alive. No more knees pressing on other peoples' necks or pernicious persons profiting from the present arrangement of things at others' expense by selfishly propping up a sickly status quo.

God is a God of movement...from hate to hope, despair to delight, captivity to freedom, and death to life!

Psalm 115

We are not seduced as the ancient Israelites sometimes were by idols crafted of metals like our psalmist describes. But we certainly are susceptible to the siren calls of contemporary idols.

When we believe money and wealth can bring us the fulfillment and security that only God can give, that is idolatry. Likewise, the pursuit of fame or reputation as the wellsprings of our self-worth is idolatrous since our true value is derived from God. Sometimes we allow our smartphones and other "screens" to assume god-like importance in our lives. St. Paul says in Philippians that, for some people, their belly is their god.

In their proper and appropriate places, the things we idolize often are commendable, enjoyable, and useful. But when they become our highest good or goal, or when we give them our first allegiance or the most attention so that ultimate fidelity to God is minimized or forsaken, then we have substituted idolatry for the divine glory and life breaks down as our relationships with God and others are diminished.

We do well to consider whether there are idols or idolatries in our lives of which we need to let go.

Psalm 116

"Precious in the sight of the Lord is the death of his faithful ones." There was a woman in the last church I served as a pastor who died after a recurring illness finally could not be kept at bay any longer. Not a longtime member of the church, nevertheless, in her six or seven years with our congregation this woman deservedly had earned the appellation "beloved."

A cancer survivor several times over, she never stopped facing outward toward the needs of others. Whether it was reading to elementary children in our inner-city schools, holding a free summer art camp in her garage for neighborhood children, or advocating for justice and peace, she took no day for granted and thanked God continually for her life and previous healings by helping to nurture the Beloved Community/kin-dom of God among us. Oh, and how she could rock a Sunday hat!

Though this psalm is a prayer of thanksgiving for recovery from an illness, it finds its complete and final fulfillment in the New Testament in the good news that we share in the glory of Christ's resurrection to new life, our final and eternal healing. Yet, in God's sight, even the deaths of faithful ones is "precious," by which the psalmist means "costly."

The death of the person I described above created a huge hole in the heart of our congregation and community. A beacon of light for the well-being of children, for the earth's protection and conservation, and for art as a means to heal our hearts and hurts, her life continued to shine even after its final earthly flicker. Mary Lou's death was costly both to God and to us, for she played a large role in our part of the body of Christ. But her death also was precious as she partakes fully now in the blessings of Christ's resurrection.

Her life had been and always will be remembered as a beautiful incarnation of the last words of this psalm: *"Praise the Lord!"* May we, too, like Mary Lou, and our psalmist, live our gratitude to God in the everydayness of our lives!

Psalm 117

Of all of the psalms in the collection of psalms, Psalm 117 is the shortest and most succinct. But its message is the heart of both the psalms and the gospel:

"Great is God's steadfast love toward us, and the faithfulness of the Lord endures forever."

In a fractured and volatile world, and in our own lives that contain their share of tumult and uncertainty, it is both a great help and a source of unlimited hope to know with surety that God will not forsake us or let us go. The good news is that even when our faithfulness to God falters, God's faithfulness to us abides.

It is not a matter of a quid pro quo. God's faithfulness to us doesn't depend on our fidelity to God. No! God is faithful. Period. But when we are faithful in response to God's grace and live graciously, our lives cohere, make sense, and have purpose. As we live in harmony with God's ways, the kin-dom of God emerges more and more in us and through us. How sweet is that?!

Hallelujah!

Psalm 118

"This is the day that the Lord has made; let us rejoice and be glad in it!"

Christian services of worship typically begin with some version of a "Call to Worship." Among those gathered, some have had good weeks, others not so good; some have borne heartaches and others have been visited by happy events. The gateway into worship is to me one of the most moving parts of the service. Whether one's week has been up, down, or somewhere in between, we all are together as one in remembering to rejoice and give thanks that we belong to the Creator who made the day, made our lives, abides with us always, and in whom we are invited to make our daily and ultimate home.

It is one thing to praise the Lord when everything is "sweetness and light," as the saying goes. It is something else altogether to praise the Lord when life's circumstances are putting us through the wringer.

But this psalmist isn't like the sports fan who is fanatical about his team so long as it is winning but who jumps off the bandwagon as soon as the team's fortunes falter.

This psalmist has suffered distress, betrayal, and reversals of many kinds and yet continues to trust that underneath, beyond, and more true than all of his troubles, is the tender, fierce, and faithful presence of God who encompasses the psalmist's life.

The psalmist knows that *nothing can separate him from the love of God.* Thus, any day is a good day to rejoice in the Lord!

A day at a time. "*This* is the day that the Lord has made; let us rejoice and be glad in it!"

Psalm 119 (Part 1)

In the last church I served as its pastor, we were fortunate to have an extremely gifted Minister of Music. Tyler was a great colleague and friend who once in a while programmed anthems, exquisite as they were, whose length strained our timing, important since our services then were broadcast on radio. Though the music always, always, was beyond compare, I would joke with him (kind of) about his occasional nine-minute anthems.

Psalm 119 is the nine-minute anthem of the Psalter. At 176 verses, it is by far the longest psalm in the collection. But it is incredibly rich. We shall take our time with it.

Five times the psalmist uses the phrase "whole heart" and another time "all my heart" to describe the standard for our commitment to God, God's Word, and the ways of God. We have to admit, if we are honest, that there are times, too many of them, when our commitment to God is less than the psalmist's ideal.

David Whyte, just before he made a career change to become a full-time poet, said one day to his spiritual director, "I'm completely exhausted." His wise friend responded, "You know, David, the antidote to exhaustion isn't necessarily rest, but wholeheartedness."

Double-heartedness is wearying. It's like having both feet planted firmly in mid-air. With the psalmist, I want to give my whole heart to God. Such a singleness of heart transforms our lives and our other relationships, and tethers us firmly within the kin-dom of God.

Psalm 119 (Part 2)

When we have a wrong-headed idea about freedom, we think it is a state of being in which we can do whatever we want to do whenever we want to do it. We do not have to listen to or consider anybody else. We are the captains of our lives and we call the shots. Having complete autonomy to live as we desire is the faux freedom we often mistakenly pursue with ultimately sad and unsatisfying results.

Autonomy is not the scriptural view of freedom. It is not what the psalmists say. Psalm 119 is the quintessential psalm for getting us in on the real nature of freedom. Freedom is living into our true and full humanity. It is the freedom to become who we really are and are meant to be in Christ. It requires discipline, perseverance, a receptive heart and mind, and love.

The revelation of God we have in scripture is not for the purpose of promulgating difficult rules that must be rigidly kept or for loading us down with limitations that restrict or constrict. The Word of God liberates us so that we are freed to love God, ourselves, and our neighbors. Repeatedly, this psalmist asserts that the precepts and commands of the Lord are our guides to freedom. Living in the way God created life to be is the real and authentic pathway to freedom.

Living in God's intended way puts us in relationship with the God behind the precepts, the same God who has made a covenant to be with us always and *whose love knows no end. That's* freedom! It is as the old hymn says, "Make me a captive, Lord, and then I shall be free..."

Psalm 119 (Part 3)

Once when a new pastoral colleague was settling into her office, she found a book that apparently had been left behind by a previous occupant. It was a strange old book to say the least. The red cover had emblazoned on it the words "Holy Bible." On the outside, it looked like a Bible. But inside the leathery cover there were about 1200 pages, all of them blank!

Was it a printer's error? Was the Bible that should have contained Genesis, Exodus, Matthew, Mark, Luke, John, the Psalms, and the rest of scripture's sixty-six books, empty by mistake?

Or was it a timely metaphor for our proclivity for making our own Bibles, for living and acting as though the only divine word is what we "write" into the Bible ourselves? Way too often, we make our own thoughts, ideas, perspectives, and even our prejudices our "scripture" instead of reading and heeding the real Holy Bible. I have a good friend who jokingly talks about a "three-ring binder Bible" into which we can put what we like and take out what we don't.

But, in Psalm 119, the psalmist says, *"Thy word (God's word) is a lamp unto my feet and a light unto my path."*

The Bible, which Christians regard as the authoritative text for our lives, instructs and illuminates the way we are to live so that we can honor God, become more fully human, and encourage the continuing formation of the Beloved Community in the world. Far from being a blank book, it is the captivating story of God's mighty acts and peoples' responses, a story in which we presently take our place. As Psalm 119 makes clear, it is a treasure filled with the wisdom and love of God.

And, thanks be to God, it is the same Word that became flesh in the person of Jesus of Nazareth.

Psalm 120

Either on a personal level or within a community, slander can be spiteful and damaging. It is a common ploy used by those who are fearful about accepting responsibility for their own complicity and culpability that has landed them in a difficult situation. In trying to save face and standing, those who slander do not care about who or what they hurt. Sometimes that hurt is severe and far-reaching.

It is easier, at least at first blush, to blame someone other than ourselves for problems of our own making. Those who are suffering by their own means demean and denigrate others to take the heat off of themselves. They create a narrative of victimhood designed to mislead and misdirect from the truth of things.

But it never finally works. Slanderers ultimately are done in by their own inglorious actions. Because slander does not carry truth, it ultimately fails in its malevolent intention to harm others.

The psalmist in his anger over someone who is slandering him creatively proposes *"a warrior's sharp arrows with glowing coals of the broom tree"* to be directed at the slanderer! In the end, though, the psalmist steps back and allows God to handle it: *"Deliver me, O Lord, from lying lips, from a deceitful tongue."* The psalmist takes heart that God is not mocked and does not allow falsehood finally to stand.

We ought neither to slander nor to worry overmuch about being slandered. There is only truth with God. The truth eventually triumphs and peace prevails. The psalmist cries out for deliverance that the Lord gladly provides.

Psalm 121

When I visit my eldest daughter, Molly, son-in-law, Joe, and grandsons, Sully and Austin, in Denver, I can see clearly the Rocky Mountains from their front porch. They rise up right before my eyes. Majestic in all seasons, they are particularly breathtaking when they are snow-capped in winter and early spring.

I never fail to call to mind this psalmist and his question whenever I see those mountains: *"I lift up my eyes to the hills - from where will my help come?"* Notice it is an interrogative rather than a declarative sentence. The psalmist does not say, "I lift up my eyes to the hills from where my help comes."

No! Greater even than the great, great Rockies is the inexpressible greatness of God who made them. The creative God who made the mountains and seas and all manner of living things is the One in whom we are invited to live and to take refuge and is the One who will help us. The psalmist assures, *"God will keep your life. The Lord will keep your going out and your coming in forevermore."*

The mountains are bold and beautiful but it is the Creator, not the creation, whom we rightly thank, trust, and praise. From where will my help come?

"From God who made heaven and earth!"

Psalm 122

This psalm begins exuberantly: *"I was glad when they said unto me, 'Let us go up to the house of the Lord!'"*

The psalmist was elated because as he and others worshiped together in the temple in Jerusalem, they sensed God's presence there, heard the Word of the Lord, received training in prayer, experienced the blessings of community and friendship, and were sent out to do justice and the things that make for peace. In good and healthy churches, the same still happens today.

In the house of the Lord in Jerusalem, the worshipers were counseled by the psalm to *"pray for the peace of Jerusalem."* Similar instruction still holds true for worshipers wherever we may be. Praying for our cities and towns is much in keeping with Jeremiah's admonition to *"Seek the welfare of the city (where you live) and pray to the Lord on its behalf, for in its welfare will you find your welfare."*

Today, the "house of the Lord" may not necessarily be bricks and mortar. I know one new congregation whose gathering place is among a grove of trees next to a river. I know of several house churches where people meet in homes. Today, the house of the Lord can be wherever people meet together in God's name. Worshiping gladly in the house of the Lord, no matter the venue, will lead us to pursue peace, justice, and equality in our towns and cities as the natural outflow of worship. As we do that, our own hearts will come to be at peace even amid the challenges and costliness of Christian discipleship.

Psalm 123

After a call to worship and an opening hymn of praise, the first part of a traditional worship service in many Christian churches is a prayer of confession. Why? *"All fall short of the glory of God."* More plainly, we are sinners. We all miss the mark of the holiness God expects and desires of us and for us.

We dare to confess our sins because "sinner" is not our primary identity. God calls us *beloved.* We are first of all God's *beloveds.* Therefore, we have a God who will not meet our confession of sin with revenge, retaliation, retribution, or reprisal. Instead, God's reaction to our sin is mercy. God meets us with mercy.

Three times in four verses our psalmist prays, *"Have mercy on us, O Lord."* "Lord, have mercy; Christ have mercy; Lord have mercy."

God responds. *"There is now no condemnation for those who are in Christ Jesus"* is the way St. Paul expresses it. We are forgiven by God and thus are freed to live into the holiness God desires for God's children. Having received mercy, it is ours, then, both to show mercy and to sow mercy whenever opportunity presents.

Psalm 124

One day my pastoral life took me to the graveside of a woman who for seventy-five years had been a member of the church I was serving at the time. Gathered there for the committal service I was leading were members of her extended family and a good company of friends.

My first words were the last words of Psalm 124: *"Our help is in the name of the Lord who made heaven and earth."* There is both good news and humbling news contained in that sentence. The humbling news is that we are not sufficient by ourselves to meet and master all of the trials, troubles, and traumas that come our way. We need assistance. The good news is that the One who *is* wholly sufficient to help us promises to abide with us. In life and in death, we belong to God.

During the service, a grandson of the deceased brought with him by pre-arrangement a speaker to plug into his smartphone so we could listen in the open air to Hilda's favorite piece of music - Judy Collins' solo rendition of "Amazing Grace." There on a chilly, windswept hill, but with the sun shining brightly, the gospel was beautifully and poignantly sung. And here's the thing that really moved my heart: as the song progressed, that little band of mourners of perhaps fifty people joined impromptu in the singing:

'Tis grace has brought me safe thus far, and grace will lead me home."

I did not see many dry eyes as we sang the hymn together. Mine welled with tears, too. We knew, we all knew, that even at the grave, maybe especially so, *"Our help is in the name of the Lord, who made heaven and earth."* Amazing grace, indeed!

Psalm 125

My youngest daughter, Emily, worked for a while after her college graduation with the Wallenda family. Yes, *that* Wallenda family! The Flying Wallendas is a group of daredevil stunt performers who engage in highwire acts *without* a safety net. Emily always has wanted to be an entertainer and at this writing is in the midst of a burgeoning acting and singing career in Hollywood. But, oh, those Wallenda days! Let's just say my prayer life intensified during that time of her post-adolescence!

Thankfully, Psalm 125 confirms that the life of faith is not similarly precarious. Just the opposite, the psalmist promised. It is firm, sturdy, solid:

"Those who trust in the Lord are like Mt. Zion, which cannot be moved, but abides forever. As the mountains surround Jerusalem, so the Lord surrounds God's people, from this time on and forevermore."

The psalm doesn't mean, of course, that Christians and other people of faith do not face risks and dangers in their lives. We meet with many of the same physical, spiritual, emotional, and financial perils and fragilities most people do. But we know they all are only penultimate because God's encompassing love is ultimate. In an earlier psalm (Psalm 30), we encountered the testimony of the psalmist assuring that though *"weeping may tarry for the night, joy comes with the morning."*

Whether that new morning comes in this life or with the resurrection dawn, our lives are, we are, eternally secure in the God *whose love knows no end.*

Psalm 126

Israel had been in servitude to the Egyptians for four hundred years but it seemed like forever. Then, at an appointed time, the Spirit of God led Moses to demand of the Egyptian Pharaoh, *"Let my people go!"* Next, as if in a dream but really happening, Moses led the people out of their bondage through a sea whose waters God parted and toward a "Promised Land" flowing with milk, honey, and freedom. The people *"were filled with laughter and shouts of joy!"*

We have had those experiences, haven't we? Times when there seemed to be no way out or no way through a difficult, sorrowful, or unjust situation and, suddenly, a way opens up, a good way. God makes ways when there appears to be no way.

"Restore our fortunes, O Lord, like the watercourses in the Negeb," the psalmist prayed. The *"watercourses in the Negeb"* were dry for much of the year until the seasonal rains fell and then, virtually overnight, the desert poured forth in blossom, bloom, and beauty.

Just so, the dry spells in our lives in love or work or creativity, at the Spirit-determined right time, spill forth with blessing and fruitfulness. *"Those who go out weeping, bearing the seed for sowing, shall come home with shouts of joy, bringing in their sheaves."*

It would be tempting to call these unforeseen events "God-surprises" except they really shouldn't be surprising. They are emblematic of how our gracious God works! *"The Lord has done great things for us!"*

Psalm 127

The meaning of this psalm isn't hidden or hard to understand. Simply put, when we try to live an autonomous life or, more accurately, when we fail to acknowledge or to count on the sustaining presence, direction, and help of God, life becomes frustrating and aggravating.

As the second half of this psalm intimates, we are, by virtue of our birth, *"a heritage from the Lord."* We are not simply children; we are children of God our Creator. Thus, reliance on God in our family life as well as in our public life is essential.

Whenever we strike out on our own and do not affirm the Lord as the cornerstone of the life we are building, we are both vain and living in vain. Whenever we attempt to build and to carry on a society without the ways of God being our foundational blueprint, we end in futility.

To announce autonomy from God, the psalmist declares, is simultaneously to proclaim our folly and foolishness. To live wisely and well is to travel the highway of our God. What can be more beautiful or satisfying than that?!

Psalm 128

What does it mean to "fear" the Lord? It's a key question because Psalm 128 says, *"Happy is everyone who fears the Lord, who walks in God's ways."*

In this context, "fear" does not mean to cower or to be afraid. The meaning of "fear" in this and other similar instances is to honor, to respect, to revere. *"Happy is everyone who honors the Lord..."*

Honoring, respecting, and revering the Lord means to live in joyful and willing obedience to God's Word and ways.

It means to refrain from installing idols like wealth, fame, or popularity in the place that rightly is God's. It means to acknowledge that our lives, and our family's life, have first, last, and foremost to do with God.

Everyone wants to be happy. Now, if only all who desire happiness would do what the psalmist describes as the condition for being truly happy - that is, to live in congruence with God's ways in the everydayness of our lives. Not only would we be more fulfilled but the kin-dom of God will grow, expand, and deepen.

"Happy, indeed, is everyone who fears the Lord, who walks in God's ways."

Psalm 129

Psalm 129 begins with ancient Israel's declaration that it has been kicked around for too long a time. The psalmist graphically describes Israel's history by declaring metaphorically, *"The plowers plowed on my back; they made their furrows long."* The psalmist recounts excruciating pain.

Yet, biblical Israel trusted the Lord to right the wrongs done against it: *"The Lord is righteous; the Lord has cut the cords of the wicked."* Paired with the previous psalm, they make it clear that in this life we experience both happiness and deep sorrow, blessings and great brokenness, hope and dire despair. Taken together, the psalms make clear that neither invalidates the other. We experience both beauty and brutality in our lives but God's salvation applies in every circumstance.

No matter our existential condition or situation, we are encouraged not to lose heart or confidence in God. We are to persevere in faith and continue to trust that God means well for us and finally will let nothing stand in the way of God's loving purposes for our lives, purposes that certainly will be accomplished (Isaiah 55:11).

Psalm 130

This psalm has everything! The efficacy of prayer from our depths, the grace of God that does not leave us condemned in our sin but bestows divine forgiveness, the sufficiency of God's Word that will never let us go as the basis on which to build a faithful life, as well as the steadfast love of the Lord, all are proclaimed and assured in the psalm's eight-verses.

When I was in college, I worked during my summer breaks on the maintenance crew of a center-city electronics manufacturing company that was housed in an old, old building. One year the plant's sprinkler system malfunctioned and a watchman was needed for several nights while the system was being repaired to be on the lookout for any fires that might break out. I was chosen to be that watchman. It was the worst job I ever had. Can you imagine how many strange and scary sounds emanated from the walls and floorboards of that ancient building? I watched more for the morning than I did for fires and was I ever glad when it came!

Just so, the psalmist said, *"I wait for the Lord, my soul waits, and in his word I hope; my soul waits for the Lord more than those who watch for the morning, more than those who watch for the morning."* Be alert! Watch! Listen! Be patient! The joy that comes from experiencing, again and again, the reality that we are "encompassed, encompassed," in the words of poet Denise Levertov, encompassed by God, is life-giving indeed! And, in Christ, morning always comes!

Psalm 131

Because the news just had come from my eldest daughter that I was going to become a grandfather for the first time, in my birth month of September no less, I took a particular interest in verse three of this four-verse psalm:

"But I have calmed and quieted my soul, like a weaned child with its mother..."

Though it was a while before my grandson was weaned, the analogy always works. Babies are very demanding and try to get their way by any means possible, but predominantly by crying. Their tears and screams mean "Get me food!" "Get me a clean diaper!" "Get me to sleep!" "Pay attention to me!" It's amazing how our littlest ones can communicate so well without words. Parent and child usually spend a fair amount of time feeling frazzled during this period of an infant's life even as love abounds.

Eventually, however, the child is weaned and settles down and delights simply in being in the loving embrace and presence of its parents. Not as preoccupied with insisting and getting, the baby more and more attunes to the parents' rhythms and the parents to their child's, and contentment sets in all around.

How wonderful it is when we are "weaned" in our relationship with God, becoming less demanding, and settling into the melody of God's grace and the harmony of God's love.

Psalm 132

"O Lord, remember in David's favor all the hardships he endured..."

Our faith comes to us courtesy of God's grace and the steadfast witness of many who came before us. They are legion who through the years have suffered persecution and even bodily injury in the service of upholding, sustaining, and spreading God's Word and ways in the world.

I am embarrassed sometimes when I hear my own and others' complaints about occasional inconveniences with which we are afflicted while seeking to serve the Lord: committee meetings that ramble on too long or a lack of appreciation by someone to whom we have provided assistance or a hymn sung in worship that we didn't like.

They all are very small potatoes compared to the martyrdom and indignities some have suffered, and still do, as they seek to live their lives in fidelity to Christ. When I think of the price others have paid for their faithfulness, the depth of their commitment to God and the gospel, and their costly obedience to Christ and his gospel, I am humbled, humbled.

Ironically, even those who have done or are doing great things for God know that the greatest gift of all is what God has done and does for us in Jesus Christ. Humility becomes us all.

Psalm 133

Psalm 133 is the psalmic precursor to the Great Prayer that Jesus prayed on the night before his crucifixion, a prayer in which he asked God that his followers all would be one in the same way that he and God were one. No doubt Jesus had this psalm in mind as he prayed for the kin-dom of God.

"How very good and pleasant it is when kindred live together in unity!" (Psalm 133:1)

Perhaps the biggest contribution the followers of Jesus can make to our nation and world is to exhibit genuine unity and show how people can live together even in the midst of profound differences. Our unity is not to be found in ironclad agreement about current issues and events, theology, politics, or practice. Our unity is in Christ whose love binds us together in common cause and amity.

It is not our divergences in points of view that pull us apart from others so much as the vitriol with which we profess them and our pride that accompanies them. It was his unity with God that made the ministry of Jesus with his disciples possible. It is, by God's grace and the ministry of the Holy Spirit, our unity with Christ, that makes possible a Beloved Community in which all persons may live together and treat all others with love, trust, and respect.

Imagine how beautiful our world could be if we allowed ourselves to live together into the fullness of such unity, if we could see God's glory in every human face!

Psalm 134

This psalm is the last in a fifteen-psalm run called the "Songs of Ascents." Starting with Psalm 120, they are the prayers the worshipers sang as they ascended the hills to get to Jerusalem on their pilgrimages to the Temple.

As such, Psalm 134 serves as a kind of benediction on the worshipers as they complete their journeys and conclude this special series of songs.

"May the Lord, maker of heaven and earth, bless you from Zion."

The benediction is to me one of the most moving elements in a Christian service of worship and the worship of many other faith traditions as well. It does far more than announce the end of the service. In the name of our triune God, the worship leader is able to bless God's people with the grace of our Lord Jesus Christ, the love of God, and the fellowship and communion of the Holy Spirit.

A benediction is not a last word. It is a first word, an enabling and ennobling word, a sending word, as we move our lives into the world anointed with the blessing of God to deal with our responsibilities, sorrows, joys, challenges, opportunities, and day-to-day necessities. What can be of more significance than God's blessing for sustaining our lives and equipping us for service in the world?

Psalm 135

Somewhere along my life's journey I heard a preacher astutely say in a sermon that "worshipers become like that which or whom they worship." I do not recall the preacher's text but it could have been Psalm 135:18.

After pointing out the idols people make with their hands or in their minds or by their actions, the psalmist offers the same observation as the preacher I heard:

"Those who make them and all who trust them shall become like them."

Most of the rest of the psalm offers reasons and examples of why God, the Holy One of Israel, should be worshiped and praised. And, truly, those who worship in spirit and in truth over the accumulation of years take on more and more of the characteristics of God...compassion, a hunger for justice and a thirst for righteousness, mercy, hospitality, kindness, generosity, and grace. Then life is blessed, the psalmist says, exclaiming at the psalm's beginning and at its end (in its original Hebrew), *"Hallelujah!" ("Praise the Lord" is its English translation.)*

Those, however, who "worship" wealth, reputation, or success as the world accounts them, technology, self-interest, social media, privilege, or any of the other idols with which we so readily fall in love, already have their temporal rewards and miss out on knowing the deeper meaning and eternal blessings of God. They miss out on the grace of knowing it is not what we have done that matters most, but what God has done and is doing in us, through us, and among us. Hallelujah! at the beginning of our day and at its end, at the beginning of our days and at their end!

Psalm 136

This psalm uses a rhetorical device known as "call and response" to convey its primary truth.

Twenty-six times various facets of God's wonderful acts in creation and history are called out. Then, twenty-six times the reason for God doing them is exclaimed: *"for God's steadfast love endures forever."* God's love for us is more than a feeling. It is more than our imagination. It is evidenced by concrete acts on our behalf.

This beautiful world God created was conceived and brought forth in love to be our magnificent home. God then acts within the history of that same marvelous creation so that opportunity and provision abound.

The litany of actions God undertook to deliver the Israelites from their bondage and servitude in Egypt are used by the psalmist as an archetypal liturgy to declare God's desire to free us, too, both communally and individually, from every unjust, unholy, or unhealthy shackle, be it physical, emotional, psychological, financial, or spiritual.

Why does God go to such great lengths for us? Because *"God's steadfast love endures forever."* And we, in our turn, stay awake and alert to what God is doing today within that enduring and steadfast love. Then, like the psalmist, we are and will be repeatedly and profoundly grateful.

♥ · ♥ · ♥ · ♥ · ♥

Psalm 137

Too many times over the years to count, I have had the rather amusing experience of someone using salty language in my presence and, when they found out I am a pastor, stumbled all over themselves in apology.

What none of them must have known is that scripture contains worse. Speaking in this psalm about the Babylonians who had plundered their homeland, destroyed their holy temple, and sent them into exile, the Judeans and Jerusalemites railed against their vanquishers, *"Happy shall they be who pay you back what you have done to us! Happy shall they be who take your little ones and dash them against the rock!"*

Not very polite, is it? Not very Jewish. Not very Christian. But, let us reconsider. The Judeans were not aiming their anger directly at the Babylonians. They were not engaging in revenge actions. They were not making a bad situation worse. *Instead, they ritualized their anger in their liturgical prayer life represented by the psalms.*

They expressed their rage to God in prayer and expected God would deal with it, comforting them while providing just desserts after a bad Babylonian meal. It wasn't the anger of the Judeans the Babylonians would face but the sovereignty of God. Just so, eventually, the exile ended and God brought the Judeans home.

Can we be as mature about our outrage? Can we let God know how we feel but trust God to sort through it all? There have been too many times I have lacked that maturity and I have regretted it each time. God greatly and deeply desires our honesty in our praying. God can handle it.

Psalm 138

This psalm contains one of the most reassuring verses in the whole collection of psalms:

"God will fulfill God's purpose for me..."

I often have heard people say they wish they could figure out "the reason God put me here." Often it's said while experiencing confusion about one's life, when life isn't going very well, when life seems stagnant, or sometimes in a new and unfamiliar season of a person's life.

But here is some pastoral counsel courtesy of the psalmist: Relax. God already is living and active in us. God already is accomplishing God's purpose in us. While we are to make good and appropriate use of our gifts, God's purpose for us goes far beyond vocational and lifestyle decisions. Our responsibility, in whatever and all that we do, is to cooperate with God by living justly, kindly, and humbly. It is, by the manner and substance of our living, to help to manifest the Beloved Community. The first question of the Westminster Shorter Catechism asks, "What is the chief end (purpose) of (humankind)?" and the answer is, "The chief end of humankind is to glorify God and enjoy God forever." God is working God's purpose out in us, Paul reminding us that God's purpose is being brought to completion in us day by day.

Because God's steadfast love endures in us, we can be confident that God's purpose for our lives will not be frustrated, but fulfilled! We cannot at every instant see it, but we may remain assured that it is so. Yet another reason in prayer and proclamation, in word and deed, to praise the Lord!

Psalm 139

"Search me, O God, and know my heart; test me and know my thoughts."

When someone truly loves us, we cherish their interest invested in us and their desire to know us completely. We do not experience their presence in our lives as intrusive, meddlesome, or unwelcome. When it is the right person, perhaps a spouse or a very trusted friend, we welcome and even find some relief in being fully known.

Even when that person has a word of rebuke or reproof for us, we believe they mean well, have our best interests at heart, and we value their wisdom. They dare to correct us or to ask us to consider their point of view precisely because of their wholehearted and well-intended love.

Just so, when we trust God's love, we do not begrudge God's involvement in our lives, but delight in it. Confident that God searches us and knows us completely, and loves us still, we are receptive to the Spirit's leading. Certain that God is for us and not against us, we do not experience God's knowing presence in our lives as disruptive or invasive, but transformative, and that is good! It is very good!

"O Lord, you have searched me and known me." And you love me all the more. The same is true for each and all of us.

Psalm 140

It is astonishing, really, the various uses that are made of power and might. Some of us first experience their misuse on the playground at the hands of bullies. I still remember as if it were yesterday a boy named Gordie who, a year or two older than I and bigger, really had it in for me for reasons I still do not know or comprehend. In elementary school years, he used his power over me to kick, punch, and humiliate me in front of others.

But, if we are honest, we have to admit that sometimes *we ourselves* as individuals are the bully, the enemy. Then, too, historically and far too often, white people have used the power of their privilege to make life unjust, unfair, and untenable for people of color, especially our Black, Brown, Asian, and Native American siblings. Wealthy people and corporations sometimes use their power and influence to promote legislation favorable to their own interests but deleterious to more vulnerable persons and communities. Nations pit themselves against other nations in ugly displays of power in order to establish their dominance and advance their own agendas.

Nothing good or helpful ultimately comes from the exercise of power in these ways.

God uses power differently. God's power is love which is mightier than all of the violent weapons ever made. God uses the power of love not to dominate, but to serve, to nurture, and *"to create in us a clean heart and to put a new and right spirit within us"* (Psalm 51). The power of love is creative and constructive, not demeaning and destructive. Says the psalmist: *"The Lord maintains the cause of the needy and executes justice for the poor."* Moreover, the power of God's love is stronger even than death. We see that most clearly in the resurrection of Jesus Christ from the dead, a resurrection in whose glory we also share!

May we use whatever power accrues to us properly and lovingly to the benefit and building up of the whole kin-dom of God!

Psalm 141

It was awful. I was eleven years old when one evening my mother was driving me and a neighbor who lived close by to a youth event at our church. I still don't know how it happened, but I forgot that Paula was in the back seat of the car and I began saying unkind (and, likely, undeserved) things about a member of Paula's family until my mother called me out and told me to stop. I recall to this day the utter horror I felt as I turned around and saw Paula's teary face. I tried to backtrack, but the considerable damage had been done.

"Set a guard over my mouth, O Lord; keep watch over the door of my lips. Do not turn my heart to any evil, to busy myself with wicked deeds in company with those who work iniquity; do not let me eat of their delicacies."

There are things we can do, options we can take, choices we can make in our lives that seem to dangle contentment and satisfaction, but they come at others' expense. Sadly, our culture often encourages us to serve our own desires and interests even if we discourage, disparage, or diminish others in the process. The psalmist's counsel: "Don't do it. Let us not eat of their delicacies."

Gossip, slander, betrayal, greed, hubris, mis-used power, and other acts and behaviors contrary to God's ways sometimes are dressed up to seem like delicacies of which we desire to partake. But they are never worth the indigestion that follows when we learn how we have harmed others, and in the long run ourselves, in the "eating" of them.

And...this counsel is as true for nations as for individuals!

Psalm 142

Most of us have had the experience this psalmist had been having of feeling invisible. It's the feeling that no one sees us or cares for us. We feel unappreciated, alone, unfairly excluded, or unduly disregarded. This can happen anytime in our lives from pre-school all the way into retirement. Thus, I resonate with a thought in a sermon I once heard in which the preacher wisely said, "Being seen feels a lot like being loved." Yes!

Notice how the psalmist handles his sad circumstance. He doesn't strike out at others. He doesn't hold pity parties for himself or sink into a sea of sorrows.

He prays. He trusts that God really is a very present help in trouble. *"Bring me out of prison,"* he says, which is how his exile from meaningful community and companionship felt to him.

God had attended to him in the past (*"When my spirit is faint, you know my way"*) and the psalmist trusts that God will do so again, and again. God will bring him into the flow of healthy and genuine community (*"The righteous will surround me, for you will deal bountifully with me"*) and the psalmist will come alive once more. He will be born anew with hope and joy.

So it shall be for us when we "take it to the Lord in prayer."

Psalm 143

Many of the psalms include complaints about, and pleas for protection from, enemies. Often, the enemies indeed are external to us. Someone is doing something to us that is not in our favor. But, other times, like the proverbial Pogo tells us, we meet the enemy and the enemy is us.

Lethargy, laziness, indifference, allowing ourselves to be carried along on the winds of peer pressure, being overwhelmed by inner thoughts and the incessant commentary about them we inflict on ourselves, the complacency of comfort, taking the course of least resistance, or doing only what feels good or expedient in the moment, we wake up one day to discover life is passing us by, that we are squandering the gifts and grace God freely gives to us.

We come to a time when our lack of accomplishment, moral fiber, meaningful work, or a loving relationship dampens our spirit and weighs us down. We discover that what we erroneously thought was freedom really has constrained and limited our lives. Meanwhile, and in contrast, God's ways of unrelenting justice, love, compassion, service, interest in others, hospitality, self-discovery, and mercy that may at first seem restrictive, painful, or too difficult become the paths to true freedom and a compelling life!

It is not too late, not ever, to change. We can join this psalmist in the humility of praying: *"Teach me to do your will, for you are my God. Let your good and gracious spirit lead me on a level path."*

Psalm 144

Psalm 144 is an example of a "royal psalm" in the Psalter attributed to one or another of Israel's kings, oftentimes David. They typically praise God and ask for divine aid in protecting Israel by subduing its enemies.

Even though we are not kings, queens, or royalty, and though by the time of the New Testament and Jesus the prayers have changed to focus on "the things that make for peace," these royal psalms, like Psalm 144, are instructive. While we do engage in spiritual warfare, we do so not by meeting evil with evil *"but by overcoming evil with good"* (Romans 12:21) with God's help.

They help us to see that the two poles of our lives are petition and praise, that just as Israel alternately prayed its needs and its thanks to God, we are invited to do so, too.

Realizing, as this psalmist says, that *"our lives are but a breath"* and *"like a passing shadow,"* we need the wisdom and help of the One who is eternal, who is *"our rock and fortress in whom we take refuge"* to live our lives well in the time accorded to us in this life. Receiving God's abiding grace, freely and lovingly given, our lives assume their appropriate orientation: gratitude.

Psalm 145

Have you ever been asked by someone to write a letter of reference and you have struggled to know what to say? Their "dossier" seems pretty thin and your challenge is to make a lot of a little. Not so of God. Not that God needs one, but Psalm 145 is the best reference letter ever written. The psalm is a *tour de force* on the nature, attributes, characteristics, and actions of God.

If you ever wonder why you should commit your life to God, Psalm 145 is your psalm. The psalmist testifies to the many reasons he is so grateful to God and why he is so desirous and eager to entrust his life to God.

"God is gracious and merciful, slow to anger and abounding in steadfast love...is good to all and God's compassion covers all that God has made...is faithful in all God's words and gracious in all God's deeds...upholds all who are falling...is just in all God's ways...is near to all who call upon God...hears our cries...watches over all who love God."

There once was a man who began to attend the church I was serving as its pastor who had been attracted by the church's mission statement. At a subsequent New Members orientation, he said to the gathered group, "I came because of what the church said about itself in its mission statement. I cried when I had been here for a while and found it all to be true. That is why I want to stay and to be a part of this congregation."

Similarly, as we commit our lives more and more to God, as we more and more "attend" to God, the more we shall come to know experientially that what this psalmist claims for God is absolutely true in its entirety!

Psalm 146

Nearing the end of our journey through the Psalms, it is obvious that one of God's primary concerns throughout this collection, as well as in the gospel of Jesus Christ, is for justice to be served for those for whom it is so often denied. It is a primary theme that recurs repeatedly in the Psalms and, later, the Gospel of Jesus Christ.

In Psalm 146, the psalmist says, *"Happy are those whose help is the God of Jacob who...executes justice for the oppressed, gives food to the hungry, and lifts up those who are bowed down."*

In the world, privilege is the chief enemy of justice. Those who seek to preserve their privilege often oppose justice for those in need of it. Those who engage in supporting voter suppression laws or gerrymandering schemes through state legislatures, for instance, are fearful of changes voters with histories, needs, and perspectives unlike their own might unleash. Those with privilege in a society who are more concerned with maintaining the present, favorable (for them) arrangement of systems are opposed to championing justice for the historically oppressed and dispossessed against whom those arrangements and systems were created and are yet arrayed. People who fear "justice for all" are afraid their world as they know it will come to an end if it happens, and so they dig in against it.

When privilege yields to prayer, as with these prayer-songs, these love songs, these psalms, our hearts will begin to be converted so that instead of greed we shall heed God's call to do justice and to love our neighbors, *all* our neighbors, as much as we love ourselves, as if our neighbors are us. Only then can we say in truth that we love God and that we praise the Lord with our whole lives, and not just our lips.

Psalm 147

Taken collectively, the last five psalms in the collection are a powerhouse of praise for the God who is our Alpha and Omega, our first and last, our all-in-all. By the time we have finished reading and praying these climactic psalms, we find ourselves in a frenzy of gratitude for everything God is, does, provides, and means to us in our lives. "Amazing grace, how sweet the sound, that saved a wretch like me..." Gloriously, by God's grace, we no longer are seen as wretches but as the beloveds of our Lord.

In this psalm, these verses particularly stand out to me: *"God's delight is not in the strength of the horse, nor God's pleasure in the speed of the runner; but the Lord takes pleasure in those who fear (honor) God, in those who hope in God's steadfast love"* (v. 10-11).

We do not have to be the strongest, fastest, smartest, wealthiest, prettiest, funniest, holiest, or most popular person in order to entice and attract God's attention and love. God loves us simply because God freely chooses to do so. God then hopes we shall see ourselves as God sees us so that we may share God's love with others in acts of kindness, justice, compassion, and friendship.

God is not so interested in how high we can climb as in how low we can stoop in order to lift others up, to serve others in ways that help them toward their full and true humanity, and that builds up the Beloved Community/kin-dom of God in the world. In doing so, we also reach toward our own deepest and truest humanity! Praise the Lord!

Psalm 148

Psalm 148 is a love song of cosmic praise! The earth has not been made solely for us human beings. All of God's creation is invited to join in a grand crescendo of euphoric acclaim of its Creator: *sun and moon and shining stars, fire and hail, snow and frost, mountains and hills, trees and wild animals, creeping things and flying birds, kings and rulers, the earth and all peoples, young and old together!*

In a day when global warming and climate change endanger the earth and all who live on it, this psalm is beyond important. It is a clarion call to befriend and to care for the whole interrelated chain of life on earth, including the earth itself. The earth is not a playground made exclusively for human beings but a delicate, intricate, and intimate home for every living thing. Indeed, we need each other - flora, fauna, sky, sea, earth, air, and humanity - in order for it truly to be well for any of us, in order for us to be complete.

We, and every part of God's creation, are made not only by God and for God but also for every other living creature and plant. We need flowers and vegetables, lakes and bees, oceans and trees, mountain streams and rain clouds as much as we need other human beings. And our non-human friends need us to live into our true humanity that cares for God's creation. We are not many creations but a single creation with many different beings all requiring the care and consideration of all for the health of all. Perhaps the chiefest of sins is to do anything to despoil the complex, elaborate, and wondrous web of life.

Therefore, the whole creation *together* is invited to sing the Creator's praise and to live in the harmony designed so graciously and sublimely by that same Creator. Praise the Lord!

Psalm 149

The psalm starts well with exuberant praise for God. But, then, the psalm seems to depict ancient Israel against the world. Talk of executing vengeance on other nations, punishing enemies, and binding others' kings in fetters and their nobles in chains of iron as an expression of the praise of God seems a far cry from the more usual psalmic declarations of joining God in bringing release to captives and doing justice on behalf of the poor, vulnerable, and powerless. Later, in the twelfth chapter of his letter to the Romans, St. Paul was to counsel against meeting evil with evil but, instead, overcoming evil with good.

Was the psalmist cheering on this small nation in its conflict against an attacking empire or did Israel have its own imperial agenda? We don't know. Most likely, the psalmist simply was saying in colorful language what God has promised all along from the very first psalm: *"The Lord watches over the way of the righteous, but the way of the wicked will perish."*

One more thing: St. Paul calls Christians *"ambassadors of reconciliation"* just as Jesus taught us to love our enemies. To seek reconciliation with our enemies, both national and personal, to love our enemies, is necessary if there is to be peace in the world, in our relationships, in our own lives, and if there is to be a more complete manifestation of the kin-dom of God among us. Too Pollyanna? I treasure what G. K. Chesterton, the British writer and Christian apologist once wrote: "It is not that the gospel has been tried and found to be wanting; indeed, the gospel has been found difficult and has been left untried."

As James said in the New Testament, *"Faith without works is dead."* We are called to gospel *living*! Praise the Lord!

Psalm 150

With Psalm 150, our journey through the Psalms concludes. There is nothing to preclude our starting over again, and I invite you to do so, because the Spirit reveals more to us every time and because we ourselves are in a different place in our lives each time we read and pray them. Thus, we are receptive in a different way. But this psalm marks the conclusion of the Psalter.

Every time I work my way through this collection of prayer-songs, I am astonished and grateful for all I discover anew about God, myself, and about the kingdom of God. I hope that has happened for you, too.

This magisterial psalm is a fitting finale to the collection. Virtually every human emotion and circumstance has been given expression somewhere in the previous 149 psalms. This psalm now gathers them all up in a symphonic praise of the God who makes all life possible and is with us in every season and situation.

Persecution, slander, betrayal, defamation, poverty, and treachery, but also compassion, kindness, mercy, humility, generosity, justice, hospitality, abundance, faith, hope, and love...they all are a part of life. From the very first psalm until the last, we are encouraged to walk not in the ways of the wicked but in the ways of God. *"Do justice, love kindness, walk humbly."* The psalms taken collectively are a love song we are invited to "sing" to God with our lips and, even more, with our whole lives even as they themselves sing to us of God's steadfast, irrepressible, and eternal love for us, a God *whose love knows no end.*

Living in the light of the sacred counsel of the Psalms, God's light, leads to a Psalm 150 world in which the great diversity of living beings celebrates together a grand unity. *"Let everything that breathes praise the Lord! Praise the Lord!"* Indeed! Amen! Yes!

Praise the Lord!

AFTERWORD

I hope you have enjoyed our journey through the Psalms. While these pages have contained my own journalings and reflections, I hope they have encouraged yours and perhaps even have led you to record them. Or, if not, maybe you will on your next time through these song-prayers! As I continue to read and pray the Psalms, I often look back on my prior journalings. Though I may be in a different place or context now than previously, and thus uncover new layers of meaning and points of contact with the Holy Spirit in my life, still it helps me to recall my earlier engagements with the Psalms, with God.

May you experience in your life both the abiding presence and abounding grace of the God the Psalms reveal and *whose love knows no end.*

~Tom

ABOUT THE AUTHOR

Thomas A. Sweet is an ordained minister, now retired, in the Presbyterian Church (U.S.A.). He graduated from the Princeton Theological Seminary and across forty-three years served gratefully and happily the Catonsville Presbyterian Church in Catonsville, Maryland; Bethel Presbyterian Church in White Hall, Maryland; First Presbyterian Church in Jamestown, New York; and Market Square Presbyterian Church in Harrisburg, Pennsylvania.

He also has preached several times from the national pulpit of the Chautauqua Institution in Chautauqua, New York.

In addition to his pastoral ministry and his special interest in the Psalms, he has been deeply involved in community and social justice ministries, believing that "faith without works is dead."

Currently residing in Harrisburg and happily involved in the Christ Lutheran Church there, he is married to Lori and, together, they are proud parents and grandparents.

In addition to his family, Sweet enjoys daily walks through woods and neighborhoods, reading, writing, meeting with friends for lunch, lingering on the nearby Gettysburg battlefield, and cheering on the Baltimore Orioles in the warm months and the Buffalo Bills in the cold ones!

If you would like to learn more or connect with the author you can visit **www.ThomasASweet.com**

www.ingramcontent.com/pod-product-compliance
Lightning Source LLC
Chambersburg PA
CBHW031126130726
47988CB00006B/2241